Artificial Intelligence and Higher Education

This book offers a comprehensive exploration of how artificial intelligence (AI) is transforming postgraduate business education in UK higher education institutions. It examines AI's evolution, applications, and ethical dimensions, integrating theoretical analysis with empirical research grounded in a critical realist and mixed-methods framework.

Through insights from students, academics, and institutional perspectives, the book highlights how AI enhances personalisation, engagement, and flexibility in learning while also raising important questions about privacy, bias, and accountability. Bridging research and practice, this work provides educators, policymakers, and researchers with a nuanced understanding of AI's pedagogical and ethical implications. It critically evaluates the opportunities and challenges of AI adoption and offers strategies for responsible and human-centred integration of intelligent technologies in higher education.

The book will appeal to scholars and advanced students in education, business, and technology—particularly those interested in higher education studies, digital transformation, and ethical AI governance. By combining conceptual insight with empirical evidence, it serves as both a theoretical foundation and a practical guide for rethinking teaching, learning, and institutional strategy in the age of AI.

Katerina Beta is Associate Dean at Global University College in Ajman, United Arab Emirates. She has over 11 years of leadership and academic experience in several countries and industries. Her research explores digital transformation and the strategic implications of emerging technologies, including AI, data analytics, and blockchain. She is particularly interested in how organisations across the public and private sectors adapt their structures, capabilities, and processes to leverage these innovations effectively.

RIOT!

Routledge Studies in Innovation, Organizations and Technology

Artificial Intelligence in Public Administration
Bożena Skotnicka-Zasadzień and Radosław Wolniak

AI, Analytics and Strategic Decision-Making
Edited by Anna Ujwary-Gil and Anna Florek-Paszkowska

The Myths of Regional Innovation
Sustainability Challenges and Responsible Innovation
Rider W. Foley

Digital Competence in Agile and Hierarchical Organizations
Operational Performance Under Global Uncertainties
Edited by Festus Adedoyin

Exploring Commercial, Social, and Digital Innovation from the Customer Perspective
Edited by Seidali Kurtmollaiev, Line Lervik-Olsen, and Tor W. Andreassen

Value Creation in Digital Platforms and Business Ecosystems
Networks, Relationships and the Platform Markets
Edited by Victoria Slettli and Sabine Baumann

Artificial Intelligence and Higher Education
The Impact of AI on Business Students' Learning
Katerina Beta

For more information about this series, please visit: www.routledge.com/Routledge-Studies-in-Innovation-Organizations-and-Technology/book-series/RIOT

Artificial Intelligence and Higher Education

The Impact of AI on Business Students' Learning

Katerina Beta

Routledge
Taylor & Francis Group
LONDON AND NEW YORK

First published 2026
by Routledge
4 Park Square, Milton Park, Abingdon, Oxon OX14 4RN

and by Routledge
605 Third Avenue, New York, NY 10158

Routledge is an imprint of the Taylor & Francis Group, an informa business

British Library Cataloguing-in-Publication Data
A catalogue record for this book is available from the British Library

ISBN: 978-1-041-12323-1 (hbk)
ISBN: 978-1-041-12324-8 (pbk)
ISBN: 978-1-003-66416-1 (ebk)

DOI: 10.4324/9781003664161

Typeset in Sabon
by Apex CoVantage, LLC

Contents

Acknowledgements

I would like to express my deepest gratitude to all those who contributed to the development of this book. My sincere thanks go to the scholars and researchers whose work has informed and inspired the chapters, as well as to the academic colleagues and MBA students who participated in the study and shared their valuable insights. I am also grateful to my peers in higher education and digital transformation for their encouragement, constructive feedback, and continued support throughout the research process. Finally, I would like to thank my family and friends for their patience, understanding, and unwavering faith in me—and above all, I am thankful to God for His grace throughout this journey.

1 Artificial intelligence and higher education

Introduction

Artificial intelligence (AI) has rapidly evolved from a theoretical concept to a transformative force in higher education, reshaping the way knowledge is created, delivered, and consumed. From its early foundations in machine learning and deep learning to the emergence of generative AI and large language models, AI has revolutionised educational systems globally. In higher education, it now supports personalised learning, intelligent tutoring, adaptive feedback, and administrative efficiency, offering universities new avenues for innovation and competitiveness. However, with these opportunities come ethical, technical, and pedagogical challenges that require critical examination. This chapter provides a comprehensive overview of AI's evolution and integration within educational contexts, highlighting its benefits, challenges, and ethical implications. It establishes the contextual foundation for understanding how AI is influencing learning experiences, particularly within UK higher education, and sets the stage for the book's subsequent exploration of its pedagogical and ethical dimensions.

Context and background of AI in education

AI is a broad and advanced term that was used on its own during the beginning of its evolution; however, between the 1980s and 2010s, the introduction of machine learning (ML) and deep learning (DL) changed the way AI systems were developed and used (Nil & Aras, 2019). After 2010, a new aspect of AI was introduced, DL, which is considered a subcategory of ML and has been developed because of the inspiration experienced by the structure and function of the brain (Marsland, 2014). Popenici and Kerr (2017) state that AI is a computing system that can engage in human-like processes such as learning, adapting, synthesising, self-correction, and the use of data for complex processing tasks. Sheikh et al. (2023) define AI as systems that display intelligent behaviour by analysing their environment and taking actions, with some degree of autonomy, to achieve specific goals. In recent years, Generative AI (GenAI) has emerged as one of the fastest-growing and embraced

DOI: 10.4324/9781003664161-1

technologies across industries and education, and it is largely driven by large language models (LLMs) (Giannakos et al., 2024).

AI has been impacting higher education systems over the last few decades with different technological developments applied to students' learning and teaching; however, at present, AI is becoming a necessity as universities are now focusing on sustainably developing the use of AI in teaching and learning to ensure that it plays an important role not only in higher education institutions but also in societies (Chan, 2023). With AI developing at a very fast pace, universities are now required to keep pace with it by creating new methods of teaching and learning. Only around three decades ago, higher education institutions were arguing about allowing even disabled students to use simple technologies such as calculators and spell-check programs (Lazarus et al., 2008). Nevertheless, only around 30 years later, education systems have significantly changed, and these technologies, powered by AI, augment students' learning and their interaction globally (Popenici & Kerr, 2017). Similarly, Chen et al. (2020) argue that AI has been broadly applied in higher education due to the development of computing and information processing techniques.

According to George and Wooden (2023), AI provides higher education institutions with a competitive advantage by reducing operational costs, reorganising and restructuring processes, and improving students' experience. Amongst the most recognised AI systems applicable in higher education are Brain–Computer Interfaces (BCIs), teacherbots, chatbots, intelligent tutoring systems (ITS), Automatic Speech Recognition (ASR), neurolinguistic programming, Smart Sparrow, and Desire2Learn (D2L). Brain–computer interfaces use brain signals and could capture and decode brain activity to enable communication and control by individuals with motor function disabilities (Osman et al., 2024). Teacherbots generally deal with automated tasks such as content delivery, basic feedback, and supervision, and they can provide a personalised teaching experience for students (Cruz et al., 2024). According to Park et al. (2022), a chatbot is defined as a robot that can communicate in real time with a large number of users through the use of a chat program. Intelligent Tutoring Systems or Intelligent Educational Systems, as they are named differently, are an AI-based technology developed and applied in higher education many years ago (Churi et al., 2022). They are based on automated tutors who possess the ability to teach mathematics, languages, science, etc. Automatic Speech Recognition and neurolinguistic programming are methods that help to sense language-related mistakes and correct them. These AI technologies assist different programs and systems mainly in the online mode of learning (Carnegie Speech or Duolingo) to provide training in foreign languages (Defrancq & Fantinuoli, 2021). Smart Sparrow is an online education platform utilised in universities in Australia. The platform assists in designing teaching content based on students' acceptance and needs (Abe, 2023). Desire2Learn (D2L) is a cloud-based learning management platform utilised mainly by higher education institutions in the

United States (Mohamed et al., 2024). The platform provides students with the opportunity to submit assignments, practise test questions, read course material, and communicate with each other. The platform is also able to analyse students' learning and then provide the necessary feedback to students and teachers. The literature review generated relevant information, mainly focusing on the challenges and benefits of AI for students learning in higher education institutions worldwide. A lack of data focusing on higher education institutions in the UK was particularly noted. The research also highlighted that there is limited research completed on the ethical implications of AI and almost no research available on how they impact students' learning (Wieczorek et al., 2025; Zainuddin et al., 2024).

Benefits and challenges of AI in education

Owoc et al. (2021) state that students benefit from AI systems which help with their exams and assignments marking process and provide quicker response and quicker feedback on their results, as well as personalised recommendations based on processing and analysing their answers. Furthermore, several AI technologies that utilise ML and natural language processing techniques help students to receive evaluations and feedback for different matters while they are studying (Alqahtani et al., 2023). Another advantage of AI for students' learning is the speed at which it receives responses. The IBM Watson cognitive computing technology has introduced chat functions that are able to answer these questions (Rajeshwari & Krishna Prasad, 2020). Using AI technology within their universities helps students not only with their learning but also familiarises them with these technologies and gains knowledge that can be applied in their future work environment (Dhawan, 2021). AI development has made a great contribution to students' collaborative learning, and it is redefining it on a scale that was not possible before, with systems and tools that connect students all around the world without the need to be physically in the same class or speak the same language. Furthermore, chatbots can help students manage their mental well-being. Another great advantage of AI for students' learning is its contribution to research. Wang et al. (2023) consider the opportunities of AI in research as exceptional, as it aids researchers to tackle complex issues, conduct experiments, and generate hypotheses. The benefits of AI have been discussed above; the following section will explore the challenges of AI in higher education institutions.

According to Kabudi et al. (2021), AI technologies and the services they offer, only provide superficial solutions and are limited to more complex endeavours of learning. AI technologies developed and used in higher education institutions provide content and material for several courses; however, although they have been used for a couple of years, they still lack flexibility and adaptability (Owoc et al., 2021). Another major issue that impacts students' learning due to AI is digital illiteracy. AI has developed very rapidly in the last few decades; however, not everyone has access to it or can understand

and use it. Students who are less aware of these technologies and lack access find it hard to use and adjust, and it is certainly worrying considering that these systems are becoming a reality in the institutions where they are studying (Rasheed et al., 2020; Dimitriadou & Lanitis, 2023).

More challenges have been highlighted to include the challenge of learning new technology, lack of technological competency, intimidation by learning new technology (Rasheed et al., 2020), confusion and resistance about looking for appropriate help online, and difficulty understanding directions and expectations while using AI systems (Mehdaoui, 2024). Application of these technologies has made learning more independent, which means that students need to manage and organise their time and learning without being told what and when to do it. This can easily lead to procrastination due to the lack of self-regulation skills (Yang & Chen, 2025).

Ethical implications of AI in education

Current research demonstrates that the ethical implications of AI can be significant; however, limited research has been conducted, and insufficient guidelines and policies have been created by institutions, organisations, and governments (Wieczorek et al., 2025; Zainuddin et al., 2024). Several ethical issues have currently been identified. White and Bradley (2022) argue that privacy is one of the biggest challenges related to AI. Data may be exposed and easily compromise security, privacy, and fairness, which then lead to ethical dilemmas. Biases can be created and expressed by algorithms, and it is a natural feature of ML and human understanding (Mavrogiorgos et al., 2024). Biases can become an issue even without the intention of the creator of the model. Moreover, AI systems that cannot be accessed by many and can be highly biased cannot be equitable. Additionally, Naik et al. (2022) argue that AI can assist the augmentation of cybersecurity; nevertheless, it can also assist the augmentation of efforts to bypass security. Lauwaert (2021) argues that those who develop AI and those who decide to deploy it should be held responsible. The lack of accountability may expose students in higher education institutions to harm and leave them suffering the consequences with no options or corrections available. Transparency, as another ethical issue of AI, ensures that accountability can be found, and privacy is not at risk by focusing on understanding when and how AI is used (Kamila & Jasrotia, 2025).

AI and higher education: why it deserves attention

Audrey Azouley, the Director-General of UNESCO, stated that AI was the biggest innovation in human history since the Palaeolithic time, during the opening keynote of the 2019 Mobile Learning Week (Tuomi, 2020). Many AI systems have been developed over the years, and their application in higher education is progressively increasing; even so, the scientific impact on learning is still unclear. There is a lack of evidence of the impact that these technologies have on learning, considering that the context of learning varies across higher education institutions, countries, and even classrooms. The author continues by stating that there is relatively scarce evidence about the benefits of AI in education. As previously stated, AI will be a game changer in education, and it will enable individuals and groups to learn remarkably better than if they were taught by a single human teacher. Furthermore, AI in higher education has the potential to transform culture, cognition, and knowledge; thus, it is becoming the primary research focus in the computer and education field (Ruano-Borbalan, 2025). On the other hand, the risks of AI going wrong in education and the psychological impact this can have on learners and teachers are huge; hence, more work needs to be done to ensure robust and safe AI products for all the stakeholders (Chaudhry & Kazim, 2022).

Chace (2020) argues that education might be the most impacted sector by AI compared to all other areas of life. The reason for this is that education is vital for students, and the current system often leaves a lot to be desired. Furthermore, the author debates that AI will transform education. AI can result in accelerating and reducing the cost of learning—even basic skills such as reading, writing, and arithmetic—on a global scale. It will make past improvements in pedagogy look like rounding errors (Chace, 2020). The author stresses the importance of education and how it will change due to AI, and states that education will become vacational instead of vocational and much more important than today. He concludes by arguing that AI will change education significantly, and when people are at a party, instead of asking each other what you do for a living, they will ask what you learn. Other authors support the above arguments by stating that AI technologies have a deep impact in education, and they are changing the relationships between teacher and students and the relationships between students in classrooms (Liu et al., 2022). Furthermore, according to Global Market Insights, in the Education Market Size, in 2020, AI exceeded $1 billion, and it is estimated to grow at a compound annual rate of 40% between 2021 and 2027 (Wiley University Services, 2022). According to the Enrolment Management Report, colleges and universities of all types and sizes will experience significant change due to AI. Considering the above context, this research focused on exploring the education sector as one of the sectors most highly impacted and changing with AI.

Furthermore, the 2019 McKinsey Global Institute Report highlights that although the USA and China are the world's powers when considering the deployment of AI, the United Kingdom is one of Europe's leaders. Additionally, the report states that the UK is more AI-ready compared to the global average, and the country can scale up its AI effort, considering its relative digital assets and competencies. The ability to capture the full potential of AI varies significantly among sectors and countries, and the United Kingdom is currently ahead of the EU-28 pack on the Artificial Intelligence Readiness Index (McKinsey Global Institute, 2019). Based on all the above assertions, the book aims to explore the impact of AI in higher education institutions in the UK. The aim will be achieved by the following three specific research objectives. This study seeks to develop a critical understanding of the AI technologies most suited to different learning modes, examining how these technologies shape the learning experiences of business postgraduate students within UK higher education institutions. It further aims to explore, through a critical lens, the ethical implications arising from the integration of AI into the higher education landscape of the United Kingdom. Finally, the research endeavours to evaluate how these ethical considerations influence and potentially transform the learning experiences of business postgraduate students in UK higher education institutions. Guided by the need to better understand the intersection of AI, ethics, and learning in higher education, this study is structured around three interrelated lines of inquiry. First, it asks how various AI technologies align with different modes of learning and in what ways they influence the learning experiences of business postgraduate students within UK higher education institutions. Second, it explores the ethical challenges and considerations that accompany the implementation of AI across these institutions. Finally, it examines how these ethical dimensions, in turn, shape and impact the learning of business postgraduate students.

Book structure

The remainder of the book is set out in the next six chapters.

Chapter 2: Artificial intelligence in higher education: tools, trends, and applications, explores the role of AI in enhancing student learning within higher education. It first introduces key concepts and the evolution of AI, clarifying its relationship with machine learning and deep learning. The second part examines the current applications of AI in universities, highlighting widely used tools, learning models, and educational theories that underpin AI-driven learning.

Chapter 3: Opportunities and challenges: the impact of AI on business postgraduate students emphasises the impact of AI on students' learning. Within this section, the challenges and benefits of AI that influence postgraduate business students' learning have been identified. Furthermore, the chapter critically explores how AI technologies are reshaping the educational experience by transforming teaching and learning practices, fostering new opportunities for personalisation, and addressing the evolving needs of modern learners.

Chapter 4: Ethical and regulatory considerations in AI-driven education examines the ethical challenges of using AI in higher education, focusing on issues such as privacy, bias, fairness, and equitable access. It notes that institutional policies and research remain limited, despite increasing AI adoption. Recent initiatives, including UNESCO's AI competency frameworks, aim to promote responsible and human-centred AI practices. The section emphasises the importance of clear policies, ongoing evaluation, and practical measures to manage ethical risks while enhancing the benefits of AI in education.

Chapter 5: Research design and methodology: a mixed-methods approach presents the research methodology used to investigate how AI affects postgraduate business students' learning in UK higher education. Using a mixed-methods approach grounded in critical realism, it combines interviews and surveys with MBA students and academics from several universities. The study adopts an inductive design, applying thematic and statistical analyses to generate new insights. Rigour and validity are maintained through triangulation, transparency, and strict ethical procedures. Overall, the chapter provides a robust methodological framework for exploring AI's impact on postgraduate learning.

Chapter 6: AI's impact on business postgraduate learning in UK higher education examines how AI influences postgraduate business education in UK universities, focusing on its impact, applications, and ethical implications. Drawing on interviews and surveys with MBA students and academics, the study finds that AI enhances learning through greater personalisation, flexibility, and accessibility, particularly via tools like STEVE, D2L, and chatbots. Despite concerns about reduced human interaction, technological dependence, and ethical issues such as privacy and bias, participants generally view AI's benefits as outweighing its risks. The chapter concludes that AI positively supports inclusive and efficient learning, provided ethical and technical challenges are effectively managed.

Chapter 7: Rethinking the future of AI in higher education: institutional strategies for responsible adoption explores how AI is reshaping higher education by enhancing personalisation, engagement, and curriculum flexibility. Recent technological advances have brought AI from research settings into classrooms, where it supports real-time feedback, adaptive learning, and student autonomy. Rather than replacing educators, AI complements their role by handling routine tasks and enabling greater focus on mentorship and guidance. The chapter also highlights ethical concerns—such as privacy, bias, and inclusivity—and calls for robust policies to ensure responsible use. Overall, AI holds great promise for improving the quality and accessibility of higher education when implemented ethically.

Conclusion

In summary, the growing presence of AI in education signifies a paradigm shift in how higher education institutions teach, learn, and operate. As AI technologies—from chatbots and intelligent tutoring systems to adaptive learning platforms—continue to advance, they offer transformative potential to personalise learning, improve accessibility, and enhance institutional efficiency. Yet, these innovations also bring forward pressing ethical concerns, including issues of privacy, bias, accountability, and equity. The review presented in this chapter demonstrates both the promise and complexity of integrating AI responsibly within higher education. It underscores the need for further research, particularly within the UK context, to better understand how AI can support postgraduate learning while maintaining human values, transparency, and trust.

Reference list

Abe, H. (2023). *Improving learning experience on the adaptive learning platforms through learning analytics and student feedback*. The University of Queensland. https://doi.org/10.14264/971f444

Alqahtani, T., Badreldin, H. A., Alrashed, M., Alshaya, A. I., Alghamdi, S. S., Bin Saleh, K., Alowais, S. A., Alshaya, O. A., Rahman, I., Al Yami, M. S., & Albekairy, A. M. (2023). The emergent role of artificial intelligence, natural learning processing, and large language models in higher education and research. *Research in Social and Administrative Pharmacy*, *19*(8), 1236–1242.

Chace, C. (2020). The impact of artificial intelligence on education. *Forbes*. Retrieved October 23, 2025, from https://www.forbes.com/sites/calumchace/2020/10/29/the-impact-of-artificial-intelligence-on-education/?sh=70fa2b7d50df

Chan, C. K. Y. (2023). A comprehensive AI policy education framework for university teaching and learning. *International Journal of Educational Technology in Higher Education*, *20*(1), 38. https://doi.org/10.1186/s41239-023-00408-3

Chaudhry, M. A., & Kazim, E. (2022). Artificial intelligence in education (AIEd): A high-level academic and industry note 2021. *AI Ethics*, *2*, 157–165. https://doi.org/10.1007/s43681-021-00074-z

Chen, X., Xie, H., & Hwang, G. J. (2020). A multi-perspective study on artificial intelligence in education: Grants, conferences, journals, software tools, institutions, and researchers. *Computers & Education: Artificial Intelligence*, *1*, Article 100005.

Churi, P. P., Joshi, S., Elhoseny, M., & Omrane, A. (Eds.). (2022). *Artificial intelligence in higher education: A practical approach*. CRC Press.

Cruz, M., Sousa, M. E., Costa, J., & Mascarenhas, D. (2024). AI-powered reconfiguration of teacher training: A case study in higher education. In *ICERI2024 proceedings* (pp. 8212–8222). IATED.

Defrancq, B., & Fantinuoli, C. (2021). Automatic speech recognition in the booth: Assessment of system performance, interpreters' performances and interactions in the context of numbers. *Target. International Journal of Translation Studies*, *33*(1), 73–102.

Dhawan, S. (2021). *Artificial intelligence in higher education: Promises, perils, and perspective*. Expanding Knowledge Horizon. OJAS, *11*, 11–22.

Dimitriadou, E., & Lanitis, A. (2023). A critical evaluation, challenges, and future perspectives of using artificial intelligence and emerging technologies in smart classrooms. *Smart Learning Environments*, *10*(1), 12.

George, B., & Wooden, O. (2023). Managing the strategic transformation of higher education through artificial intelligence. *Administrative Sciences*, *13*(9), 196.

Giannakos, M., Azevedo, R., Brusilovsky, P., Cukurova, M., Dimitriadis, Y., Hernandez-Leo, D., Järvelä, S., Mavrikis, M., & Rienties, B. (2024). The promise and challenges of generative AI in education. *Behaviour & Information Technology*, 1–27. https://doi.org/10.1080/0144929X.2024.2394886

Kabudi, T., Pappas, I., & Olsen, D. (2021). AI-enabled adaptive learning systems: A systematic mapping of the literature. *Computers and Education: Artificial Intelligence*, *2*, 100017.

Kamila, M. K., & Jasrotia, S. S. (2025). Ethical issues in the development of artificial intelligence: Recognizing the risks. *International Journal of Ethics and Systems*, *41*(1), 45–63.

Lauwaert, L. (2021). Artificial intelligence and responsibility. *AI & Society*, *36*(3), 1001–1009.

Lazarus, S., Thurlow, L., Lail, E., & Christensen, L. (2008). A longitudinal analysis of state accommodations policies: twelve years of change, 1993–2005. *The Journal of Special Education*, *43*(2), 67–80. Doi: 10.1177/0022466907313524

Liu, Y., Chen, L., & Yao, Z. (2022). The application of artificial intelligence assistant to deep learning in teachers' teaching and students' learning processes. *Frontiers in Psychology*, *13*, 929175.

Marsland, S. (2014). *Machine learning, an algorithmic perspective* (2nd ed., pp. 4–5). Chapman and Hall/CRC.

Mavrogiorgos, K., Kiourtis, A., Mavrogiorgou, A., Menychtas, A., & Kyriazis, D. (2024). Bias in machine learning: A literature review. *Applied Sciences*, *14*(19), 8860.

McKinsey Global Institute. (2019). *Artificial intelligence in the United Kingdom: Prospects and challenges*. Prepared for London Tech Week, June 2019, in collaboration with QuantumBlack and McKinsey & Company UK and Ireland.

Mehdaoui, A. (2024). Unveiling barriers and challenges of AI technology integration in education: Assessing teachers' perceptions, readiness and anticipated resistance. *Futurity Education*, *4*(4), 95–108.

Mohamed, M. E., Oliveira, H. C., Biswas, S., & Moussa, A. (2024). Orchestrating optimal blended learning in theoretical courses: A framework for enriching education. *International Journal on Innovations in Online Education*, *8*(1), 1–18.

Naik, B., Mehta, A., Yagnik, H., & Shah, M. (2022). The impacts of artificial intelligence techniques in augmentation of cybersecurity: A comprehensive review. *Complex & Intelligent Systems*, *8*(2), 1763–1780.

Nil, G., & Aras, B. (2019). Artificial intelligence in education: Current insights and future perspectives. In *Handbook of Research on Learning in the Age of Transhumanism* (pp. 224–236). IGI Global.

Osman, N. M., Refai, M. K., Elshafey, K., & Ayoub, B. M. (2024). A literature review of bcis for assisting scis with disabilities from a developmental point of view and potential future trends. *Journal of Al-Azhar University Engineering Sector*, 53–83.

Owoc, M., Sawicka, A., & Weichbroth, P. (2021). *Artificial intelligence technologies in education: Benefits, challenges and strategies of implementation*. http://www.ue.wroc.pl/en/

Park, D. M., Jeong, S. S., & Seo, Y. S. (2022). Systematic review on chatbot techniques and applications. *Journal of Information Processing Systems*, *18*(1).

Popenici, S., & Kerr, S. (2017). Exploring the impact of artificial intelligence on teaching and learning in higher education. *Research and Practice in Technology Enhanced Learning*, *12*(1), 1–13.

Rajeshwari, M., & Krishna Prasad, K. (2020). IBM Watson industry cognitive education methods. *International Journal of Case Studies in Business, IT, and Education (IJCSBE)*, *4*(1), 38–50.

Rasheed, R. A., Kamsin, A., & Abdullah, N. A. (2020). Students and teachers' challenges of using technology in blended learning environments. In *Proceedings of the 2020 the 3rd international conference on computers in management and business* (pp. 195–200). ACM Digital Library.

Ruano-Borbalan, J. C. (2025). The transformative impact of artificial intelligence on higher education: A critical reflection on current trends and futures directions. *International Journal of Chinese Education*, *14*(1), 2212585X251319364.

Sheikh, H., Prins, C., & Schrijvers, E. (2023). Artificial intelligence: Definition and background. In *Mission AI: Research for policy*. Springer. https://doi.org/10.1007/978-3-031-21448-6_2

Tuomi, I. (2020). *The use of artificial intelligence (AI) in education*. Research4 Committes. Retrieved October 23, 2025, from https://research4committees.blog/2020/09/07/the-use-of-artificial-intelligence-ai-in-education/

Wang, H., Fu, T., Du, Y., Gao, W., Huang, K., Liu, Z., Chandak, P., Liu, S., Van Katwyk, P., Deac, A., Anandkumar, A., Bergen, K., Gomes, C. P., Ho, S., Kohli, P., Lasenby, J., Leskovec, J., Liu, T.-Y., Manrai, A., . . . Zitnik, M. (2023). Scientific discovery in the age of artificial intelligence. *Nature*, *620*(7972), 47–60.

White, R., & Bradley, D. (2022). Artificial intelligence, ethics and privacy. In *EcoMechatronics: Challenges for evolution, development and sustainability* (pp. 129–152). Springer International Publishing.

Wieczorek, M., Hosseini, M., & Gordijn, B. (2025). Unpacking the ethics of using AI in primary and secondary education: A systematic literature review. *AI Ethics*, *5*, 4693–4711. https://doi.org/10.1007/s43681-025-00770-0

Wiley University Services. (2022). *5 ways artificial intelligence may influence higher education admissions and retention*. Retrieved October 23, 2025, from https://universityservices.wiley.com/artificial-intelligence-in-higher-ed-admissions-retention/

Yang, Y., & Chen, L. (2025). A study on the influencing factors of online learning procrastination of English learners based on artificial intelligence. *International Journal of High Speed Electronics and Systems*, *34*(02), 2440045.

Zainuddin, N., Suhaimi, N. A., Jaffar, M. N., Norwawi, N. M., Sahrir, M. S., Wan Daud, W. A., & Abdul Ghani, M. T. (2024). Responsible and ethical use of artificial intelligence in language education: A systematic review. *Forum for Linguistic Studies*, *6*(5), 316–325. https://doi.org/10.30564/fls.v6i5.7092

2 Artificial intelligence in higher education

Tools, trends, and applications

Introduction

AI has become one of the most transformative forces shaping higher education in the twenty-first century. Once a theoretical concept confined to research laboratories, AI now permeates everyday academic practices, redefining how students learn, how educators teach, and how institutions operate. This chapter explores the evolution, tools, and applications of AI in higher education, focusing on how technological innovation intersects with pedagogy to create adaptive, efficient, and inclusive learning environments. It examines AI's conceptual foundations—tracing its relationship with ML and DL—while analysing its growing presence in universities worldwide through tools such as intelligent tutoring systems, chatbots, and adaptive learning platforms. The discussion also considers how AI connects with learning theories and pedagogical paradigms to enhance student engagement and autonomy. By mapping current trends, opportunities, and challenges, the chapter provides a comprehensive understanding of AI's expanding role in higher education and its potential to redefine the future of learning.

An overview of AI

The term "artificial intelligence" was first proposed by John McCarthy in the mid-twentieth century at the Dartmouth Conference (Zhang & Lu, 2021). John McCarthy, considered as the father of artificial intelligence, in 1956, provided the first and most influential explanation of AI, defining it as the study of AI to proceed based on the conjecture that every aspect of learning or any other feature of intelligence can in principle be so precisely described that a machine can be made to simulate it (Russell & Norvig, 2010). Since then, scholars have provided different definitions of AI, which have changed over the years due to the rapid development of the technology. Almost four decades later, in the 1990s, McCarthy defined AI as the science and engineering of making intelligent machines, especially intelligent computer programs (Minsky et al., 2006). Both definitions are similar, given that McCarthy focuses on the making of intelligent machines that can simulate any aspect of

DOI: 10.4324/9781003664161-2

intelligence as the basis of AI. Subsequently, many definitions from the 2000s until nowadays have been identified.

Nabiyev (2010) describes AI as the capability of a device controlled by computers to accomplish tasks in the same way as humans do, such as reasoning, generalisation, learning from past experiences, and making meaning. Badaró et al. (2013) define AI as the best way to simulate the human brain's intelligence capabilities. On the other hand, Nilsson (2014) refers to AI as the entirety of an algorithmic construction copying human intelligence, where raw data, received from any user, is filtered by a device, made meaningful, and processed before finally becoming cooked data capable of meeting the demands of users. According to Deng (2018), AI is a technology of computer science that aims at the development of algorithms, methods, and theories as well as applications that simulate human intelligence. The author argues that AI helps to move from a world where computers receive rules from humans to provide solutions to problems, to a world where algorithms help machines to solve problems on their own without human guidance. Harkut and Kasat (2019) state that AI is the simulation of human intelligence processes by machines, especially computer systems, and therefore it is a set of computational techniques inspired by the way humans use their nervous system and their body to feel, learn, and act. In 2019, another definition of AI was provided by Huang et al. (2019), who identify it as the study of how computers can perform intelligent tasks, which in the past were only accomplished by humans.

Recently, AI has been defined by numerous authors and scholars. Gupta et al. (2021) consider AI as the ability of computer systems to learn from past data. Furthermore, Xu et al. (2021) argue that AI stimulates human intelligent behaviours through the use of computers, which are trained to learn human behaviours such as judgement, learning, and decision-making. Xu et al. (2021) discuss that AI aims at developing machines that think like humans and copy human behaviours such as learning, perceiving, predicting, planning, reasoning, etc. On the contrary, Crawford (2021) argues that AI is neither artificial nor intelligent; the author defines AI as embodied and material, made from natural resources, fuel, human labour, infrastructures, logistics, histories, and classifications; and that AI systems are not autonomous, rational, or able to discern anything without extensive, computationally intensive training with large datasets or pre-defined rules and rewards. More recently, Accenture (2022) argues that AI is a constellation of many different technologies working together to enable machines to sense, comprehend, act, and learn with human-like levels of intelligence. Sheikh et al. (2023) define AI as systems that display intelligent behaviour by analysing their environment and taking actions, with some degree of autonomy, to achieve specific goals. In recent years, GenAI has emerged as one of the fastest-growing and embraced technologies across industries and education, and it is largely driven by large language models (Giannakos et al., 2024).

Quinn and Goldstraw-White (2022) classify AI into three categories: artificial narrow intelligence (ANI), artificial general intelligence (AGI), and artificial superintelligence (ASI). The ANI has a narrow range of abilities; the AGI is on par with human capabilities, whereas ASI is more skilled than humans. He argues that to date, only ANI has been successfully realised. Similarly, Agnihotri (2022) discusses that narrow AI, which is also known as weak AI, is the most successful and widely used category of AI. It can perform a single specific task within a limited context and excel in one particular function without being generalised to perform the tasks. On the other hand, general AI allows machines to compete with human intelligence by thinking abstractly, strategically, and creatively. Even though they can perform some tasks better than humans, general AI is still not fully realised and does not yet exist outside the silver screen (Accenture, 2022). This classification of AI has also been considered by Lateef (2022). The author argues that narrow AI or weak AI allows machines to perform a narrowly defined set of specific tasks; general AI or strong AI will allow machines to think and make decisions like humans, and artificial superintelligence will allow machines to surpass human intelligence.

Another classification of AI has been considered based on the machine's likeness to the human mind. Joshi (2019) states that based on this criterion, AI machines have been classified into the following categories: reactive machines, limited memory machines, theory of mind, and self-aware AI. Reactive machines are the oldest versions of AI machines with very limited capabilities and no memory, which only respond to different stimuli. Similarly, Marr (2021) argues that reactive AI functions based on the input received, and it is programmed with a predictable output to respond in the same way to identical situations without being able to learn or perceive the past or future. On the other hand, even though limited memory machines have the same capabilities as reactive machines, they are capable of making decisions based on learning historical data. Almost all current AI tools and systems are driven by limited memory (Tănăse et al., 2024). Similarly, Betz (2022) discusses that limited memory machines can store knowledge and use it for future tasks. Johnson (2020) also considers that limited memory machines are more complex than reactive AI machines and use data to make better predictions.

Conversely, theory of mind and self-aware AI are two types that currently exist only as concepts or as work in progress. Theory of mind AI will better understand the needs, beliefs, emotions, and thought processes of the entities it interacts with. Whereas self-aware AI, which currently only exists hypothetically, will be fully self-aware, not only understanding others' emotions, needs, beliefs, etc., but also having its own needs, beliefs, thoughts, and desires (Tănăse et al., 2024). Theory of mind artificial intelligence machines will be able to understand people's emotions and thoughts, and influence the machine's thought process to identify and remember emotional output and behaviours, and know how to respond to them. Furthermore, Petterson (2021) discusses that this type of AI is not yet realised, and it will be capable of understanding human reasoning and delivering personalised solutions and results based on needs and motives. Self-aware AI, on the other hand, is considered unlikely to be achieved at the present circumstances; nevertheless, this stage of superintelligence can be achieved in the future (Lateef, 2022). Similarly, Agnihotri (2022) argues that self-aware AI is the highest goal of AI, where machines possess their own awareness and representation of the world and do not need to borrow consciousness from a model.

Evolution of AI

AI is a concept that dates back to the 1950s and has experienced a history of more than 70 years (Zhang & Lu, 2021). According to Popenici and Kerr (2017), Alan Turing attempted to answer the question of when a system that is designed by humans can be considered intelligent, and suggested testing a human by distinguishing a conversation with another human or with a machine. If the human listener could not distinguish between the two, then the system could be considered intelligent and called AI. In 1956, at the Congress of Information Theory in Massachusetts, Noam Chomsky established the language parameters. Language similar to mathematics referred to a system that is structured systematically under a formal scheme, which justified the attribution of human capacities to a machine, considered a form of mechanical thinking in a computer. Based on the analysis of this proposal, two ways of understanding AI were created: a weak AI, which studies the cognitive possibilities of the human being through the use of computers only, and a strong AI, which focuses on connecting AI with human intelligence (Eschker & Liu, 2024).

The 1956 Dartmouth Summer Research Project on Artificial Intelligence marked a pivotal moment in defining AI as the attempt to formalise and replicate human intelligence in machines. It introduced the idea that both computers and human minds process information similarly, using data and formal rules to solve problems and make decisions. After the workshop in 1956, this proposal became the leading approach, and the researchers of AI began to study the developments of intelligent human behaviour to be able to reproduce that behaviour by automated means (Dick, 2019). Nowadays, however, the main concepts and approaches of AI that were introduced at its beginning are abandoned and remain just symbolic. The rationale behind that is that in its early times, AI was strongly related to human intelligence, as its main goal was to reproduce intelligent human behaviours in machines; however, currently the main focus is to produce automated systems that perform well by utilising any resources, not necessarily humans.

First wave of AI

The first wave of AI is called Internet Artificial Intelligence and is characterised by algorithmic systems that were fed by masses of user data to curate online content. During the first wave of AI, which began in the 1960s, the experts of AI at that time designed these systems based on knowledge that was quite helpful in providing solutions for narrow-domain problems by exploring the most relevant parameters and providing a resolution about the best action to take for each condition (Sheth & Thirunarayan, 2021). The author states that the main strength of these first-generation AI systems was their clear and understandable way of performing basic logical reasoning. During the 1970s and 1980s, expert systems developed further, and the speech recognition approach became very popular. Nevertheless, there were numerous limitations related to the functionality of the systems, with the main problem arising from the difficulty to learn algorithmically from information and data and of handling uncertainty in reasoning in the knowledge-based approach. Likewise, Rüfenacht (2020) considers Internet Artificial Intelligence to have reached us all with machines that use algorithms to detect behaviour patterns and provide personalised content.

Second wave of AI

The second wave of AI, or Business Artificial Intelligence/Agentic AI, began in the 1980s, and it was primarily based on ML. These systems' performance was better than the knowledge-based system, which operated during the first wave; however, even though there were improvements compared to the first wave, the systems created during the second wave were still not comparable to human performance (Wu et al., 2025). The main limitation of the second wave was related to a lack of deep representations of data and insufficient capacity to absorb huge amounts of data because of the lack of power of the algorithms and computing infrastructures. The second wave allowed algorithms to be trained on exclusive data sets ranging from simple processes to more complex business processes. Business Artificial Intelligence uses structured data to optimise and generate value and is capable of generating immense and rewarding opportunities and impacting the way people work (Cristofaro & Giardino, 2025).

Third wave of AI

The third and current wave of AI, or Perception Artificial Intelligence, dates roughly around 2010. This wave is characterised by a DL paradigm, which breaks away difficulties faced during the first and second waves. The development of DL is the main force that drives a big growth of AI nowadays, as well as the advancements of neural networks (Deng, 2018). Throughout this wave, DL has significantly affected speech recognition, which is the first real-world AI application. Speech recognition is not the only AI application that has been affected by DL; other real-world applications have become successful because of DL (Felt & Irwin, 2024). Examples include image captioning, web search, visual question answering, natural language processing, customer relationship management, internet adverts, board games, robotics, medical image analysis, etc. Perception Artificial Intelligence is about giving machines senses and thus opening up the spectrum for context. Zaraki (2020) discusses that Perception Artificial Intelligence allows machines to understand the features, facts, and context and not simply categorise and detect but is capable of providing reasons behind the decision made.

Fourth wave of AI

The fourth wave of AI, or Autonomous Artificial Intelligence is a wave that enables AI to act productively and allows the machines to sense and respond to the world around them (Rüfenacht, 2020). The fourth wave of AI aims at creating systems that operate completely autonomously, without human intervention; however, this wave is the most difficult to assess in its development, considering that the autonomous systems should be able to respond to changes and cope with irregularities and deviations. Autonomous Artificial Intelligence can move intuitively and manipulate objects similarly to humans. The fourth wave of AI, or Purposeful Artificial Intelligence, is a wave where technology is leveraged to amplify people by automating all repetitive tasks and freeing them to use their passion and creativity to think about bigger opportunities (Wu et al., 2025).

Artificial intelligence, machine learning, and deep learning

AI is a broad and advanced term that was used on its own during the beginning of its evolution; however, between the 1980s and 2010s, the introduction of ML and DL changed the way AI systems were developed and used (Nil & Aras, 2019). In 1959, Arthur Samuel stated that ML is a field of study where computers are given the ability to learn without being fully programmed; simply put, it is a way of achieving AI (Marsland, 2014). According to Badillo et al. (2020), ML has been described as the primary AI application; on the other hand, others consider it a subset of AI. Zhang and Lu (2021) consider ML as the science of AI, which uses data or experience to optimise the performance standards of computer programs. ML helps to train an algorithm by using a huge amount of data, thus allowing the algorithm to learn, improve, and solve different problems such as regression, segmentation, classification, and network analysis. ML has developed as part of AI as a method of choice with the intention of developing diverse software and applications, such as software for computer vision, natural language processing, speech recognition, robot control, etc. ML allows machines to learn without being explicitly programmed by inputting data along with algorithms (Taye, 2023).

After 2010, a new aspect of AI was introduced, DL. DL is a subcategory of ML and has been developed as a result of the inspiration experienced by the structure and function of the brain. This new complex technology strives to understand and solve perception and cognition at the human level. DL is a specialised subset of ML that utilises layered neural networks to automatically learn hierarchical representations of data. These models capture complex patterns by progressively building abstract concepts from simpler ones, enabling them to perform tasks like image recognition, natural language processing, and autonomous decision-making (Taye, 2023). DL combines low-level features to form high-level attribute categories through the distribution characteristics of data. It is a subset of ML, which in itself is a subset of AI; thus, the evolution goes like this: AI > ML > DL.

The development of AI, ML, and DL led to the development of AI systems based on algorithms that learn from and make predictions on data. Limna et al. (2022) argue that as a result of these developments, AI has already entered the education sector, and it is being increasingly used in higher education institutions. Consequently, the next section discusses the current applicability of AI in these institutions.

AI in academia: essential tools and applications

When studying the impact that AI has in higher education institutions (HEIs), Popenici and Kerr (2017) state that AI is a computing system that can engage in human-like processes such as learning, adapting, synthesising, self-correction, and the use of data for complex processing tasks.

Huang et al. (2019) argue that AI has developed rapidly in recent years, and it has changed people's lifestyles. AI has been impacting higher education for a couple of decades with different technological developments applied for students' learning and teaching; however, nowadays this is not limited to education only, and AI is becoming a necessity while universities are highly focusing on sustainably developing to play an important role in societies (Aldosari, 2020). With AI developing at a very fast pace, universities are now required to keep pace with it by creating new methods of teaching and learning. Similarly, Ouyang and Jiao (2021) argue that AI has been widely applied in higher education since the development of computing and information processing techniques and provides new opportunities, challenges, and potentials in educational practices. According to Limna et al. (2022), implementing AI in higher education is a critical and strategic factor in educational development. Several AI systems have already been applied in different institutions around the world, affecting the way teaching is taking place, the way students are learning, and the way the institution itself is operating. The focus of innovation in education should not be just about introducing more technology into class, but it should be about ensuring that approaches to teaching are changing, and students can benefit by obtaining and enhancing skills that will help them succeed in competitive environments (Chan &

Tsi, 2023; Strielkowski et al., 2025). Some of the AI systems implemented and used in higher education institutions are described as follows.

Brain–computer interfaces (BCIs) and teacherbots

Brain–computer interfaces (BCIs) are an AI development, which, by using brain signals, can capture and decode brain activity in order to enable communication and control by individuals with motor function disabilities (Alimardani & Hiraki, 2020). In higher education institutions, BCIs are used to check students' focus on the content and the tasks. On the other hand, teacherbots can play the role of a teacher throughout the duration of a course. Teacherbots are currently dealing generally with automated tasks such as content delivery, basic feedback, and supervision, and they can provide a personalised teaching experience for students (Pillai et al., 2024). At the University of Georgia Tech in the USA, Jill Watson (the teacherbot) was teaching in the online master's programme and was nominated by the students as the best teaching assistant due to her ability to meet students' expectations to high levels. The nomination was done by the students without them knowing that Jill Watson was a teacherbot and not a real person. Teacherbots, as a very important AI development, have already become a disruption to traditional teaching staff.

IBM's supercomputer Watson

IBM's supercomputer Watson, as an example of a teacherbot, is one of the systems created through ML. It is currently utilised at Deakin University in Australia, and it provides students with advice 365 days a year (Neeharika & Riyazuddin, 2023). It is also used in a number of universities around the world, such as the United States and Canada, and particularly at Rensselaer Polytechnic Institute, Pennsylvania State University, Pomona, UMBC, and the University of Ottawa. Watson's computer functions based on algorithms and inputted data to respond and fulfil repetitive, predictable tasks. As the system always provides advice for students, it can affect their learning in a positive way, due to the ability to get responses quicker instead of waiting for an answer from a human being who might only be available for a limited amount of time. Watson's disadvantages are typically related to its ability to only answer certain questions and the inability to provide solutions to more complex situations, providing mostly superficial solutions (Ali, 2025). Nevertheless, a decade later, Watson has improved its capabilities and is competing with the big three tech cloud providers, Amazon, Google, and Microsoft. The Allen Institute of Artificial Intelligence compared the performance of Watson on natural language tasks, such as identifying places, persons, and sentiments of sentences, with the services provided by them and found that Watson did as well or better than the big three (Lohr, 2021).

Chatbots and virtual agents

Chatbots and intelligent/virtual agents are other AI-based technologies utilised in several higher education institutions by students. The chatbot is defined as a robot that can communicate in real time with a large number of users through the use of a chat program. Chatbots generate an outstanding optimisation of the user's experience and can request possible solutions for several problems that users might experience (Park et al., 2022). Ada chatbot, developed in 2016 and used at Bolton College in England, answers students' questions about the college and also more personalised questions such as "What is my grade" or "What is my timetable" (Jisc, 2022). Furthermore, the Becky chatbot was developed and used at Leeds Beckett University in 2017 to help students through clearing by taking them through the whole application process and by making offers (Jisc, 2022). Alternatively, virtual agents are considered to be intelligent personal assistants that can execute tasks and offer services to students in real time through voice-controlled technology. Virtual agents are able to adjust teaching methods by creating a customisable experience for students and assist them with the areas of improvement (Yadav et al., 2023). An example where chatbots and virtual agents are collectively used to provide a better and more interactive learning experience for students is the Dutch institution Avans Applied Science University. A simulation game was created by a law teacher to train students in handling a bankruptcy case with the help of a chatbot and a virtual agent, which ask legal questions to students and interact with them to solve the case (Avans University of Applied Sciences, 2022).

Intelligent tutoring systems (ITS)

Intelligent tutoring systems or intelligent educational systems, as named differently, are an AI-based technology developed and applied in higher education many years ago, since the 1980s when Lego Mindstorms was developed by the ITM Media Lab (Ocaña-Fernandez et al., 2019). They are based on automated tutors who possess the ability to teach mathematics, languages, science, etc. The use of ITS in universities has boosted online learning and, therefore, provided students with the ability to study from all over the world without the need to move to a particular country and university, in addition to addressing students' diverse learning needs and styles. Spice (2020) argues that tutoring systems are capable of tracking students' performance continually, providing feedback and suggestions related to the next steps, and helping students to learn new skills through practice problems. ITS have been used for several years; however, during the last decade, they have become richer and more robust in having life-like personas, attempting to simulate human capacities, tracking how attentive students are, detecting feelings, and teaching physical motor skills (Lin et al., 2023; Alrakhawi et al., 2023). They are created in different ways and may appear visually, with sound or text, as animations, humans, or personified robots. They focus on producing superior learning outcomes by responding to students in a very similar way to humans, mastering inflection and facial expressions, and nurturing connection and engagement emotionally and socially (Schiff, 2021). Moreover, they possess the ability to take on different roles such as teacher, assistant, companion in learning, tutor, etc., and they can be differentiated based on their emotional attitude as firm and commanding, neutral, or very sensitive and by activity, from direct teaching to guidance to collaborative learning (Schiff, 2021). Intelligent tutoring systems created with AI technology are focusing increasingly on their ability to collaborate and interact with students, making them think and feel that the material is not challenging, and increasing their enthusiasm and consideration. According to Cao et al. (2021), students' acceptance of using intelligent tutoring systems in higher education institutions in China increased during the COVID-19 pandemic due to perceived ease of use and perceived usefulness of these systems. Another example of the application of ITS in higher education is AutoTutor, developed and used at the University of Memphis in the United States. The ITS operates through a naturalistic dialogue with the students and is able to generate complex problems and assist students through a back-and-forth type of communication to find solutions, mainly in the field of math and science (Cameron, 2021).

Soar Training Expert for Virtual Environments (STEVE) and Agent for Distance Education: Light Edition (ADELE) are two examples of ITS, developed and used at the USC Information Sciences Institute in Southern California. STEVE monitors the condition of the virtual setting and manipulates it through virtual motor actions. It can show and explain to students how to complete physical and procedural tasks, assist and instruct them as necessary, and can become a team member when the team requires training (Goenka et al., 2021). Besides, STEVE focuses on creating a collaborative environment for students by not only demonstrating the tasks but also monitoring the students' performance after the task's completion. ADELE supports students to work through problem-solving exercises, both one-to-one tutoring and collaborative exercises. The agent interacts with the students by monitoring their actions and providing feedback, suggesting correct actions, providing hints for particular actions, and providing contextual assessment to test students' understanding and help them improve. The main focus of STEVE and ADELE is to create a collaborative environment for students with the purpose of appearing lifelike and interacting on an ongoing basis (Goenka et al., 2021).

Automatic speech recognition (ASR) and neurolinguistic programming

Automatic speech recognition (ASR) and neurolinguistic programming are methods that help to sense language-related mistakes and correct them. These AI technologies assist different programs and systems mainly in the online mode of learning (Carnegie Speech or Duolingo) to provide training in foreign languages (Ocaña-Fernandez et al., 2019). These techniques assist students at universities when learning foreign languages as part of their study programmes. University College London Medical School is one of the higher education institutions that uses automatic speech recognition (UCL, 2022). Furthermore, the University of Sheffield developed one of the world-leading systems for large vocabulary automatic speech recognition, which won the international evaluation campaigns for rich speech transcription, a competition organised by the US National Institute of Standards and Technology (NIST), in both 2007 and 2009 (Research Excellence Framework, 2014). The neurolinguistic programming method is used in universities all around the world. The University of California is an example of the application of this AI method. Furthermore, neurolinguistic programming knowledge is also shared with students through several available modules in several universities, such as Bircham International University in Spain (Bircham International University, 2022), College of Management and IT in Ireland, E-Careers in Australia, Lund University in Sweden (IDP, 2022), Oxford Learning College in England (Oxford Learning College, 2022), etc.

Smart Sparrow

Smart Sparrow is another AI-powered technology already applied in higher education institutions. Smart Sparrow is an online education platform utilised in universities in Australia. The platform assists in designing teaching content based on students' acceptance and needs (Wan, 2020). The platform offers a rich, interactive, and adaptive educational content and learning experience for students that stimulates engagement and better learning outcomes in several fields of study, such as science, engineering, medicine, etc. (Hoboken, 2020). Additionally, Smart Sparrow offers a great number of simulation experiments, such as designing virtual buildings and complex virtual surgeries, to allow students to "learn by doing". Smart Sparrow was invented and used at the University of New South Wales in Sydney, Australia, and nowadays is used by over 700 leading institutions across K-12, higher education, and corporate (Smart Sparrow, 2022).

Desire2Learn (D2L)

Desire2Learn (D2L), also known as Brightspace, is a cloud education learning management platform utilised by higher education institutions in the US (Bai, 2022). The platform provides students with the opportunity to submit assignments, practise test questions, read course materials, and communicate with each other. The platform is also able to analyse students' learning and then provide the necessary feedback to students and teachers. The feedback provided is beneficial for students, as it allows them to understand their current progress and the areas for improvement. Furthermore, the platform can assist students in making the right choices by predicting which courses are suitable for each of them. Many higher education institutions use D2L as a learning management platform for students. Examples of these institutions include University College Dublin in Ireland, Aarhus University in Denmark, Tshwane University of Technology in South Africa, Amsterdam University of Applied Sciences in the Netherlands, University of Suffolk in England, and many more (D2L, 2022).

Adaptive learning systems

Adaptive learning systems are some of the most mature AI-powered education technology systems, which change the level, pace, and order of learning based on algorithms and adapt the learning experience to suit the learners (Jisc, 2022). They are mostly suitable for courses where clearly defined and step-by-step knowledge is available, and allow students to learn at their own pace. The systems test students' level of knowledge and afterwards can suggest the next step based on the results. Kabudi et al. (2021) argue that advanced adaptive learning systems developed recently can deliver learning content and adapt to students' individual needs. An example of an adaptive learning system includes the Biospine adaptive learning system, developed in 2019 at Arizona State University. Biospine provides an online experience responsive to students' needs, where learning activities are linked, and students can progress through their assignments based on their knowledge level. It also allows students to step back if they need to and cover certain knowledge repeatedly until they are ready to move on to the next step (Jisc, 2022). Pappas and Giannakos (2021) also suggest that adaptive learning systems assist educators in revising the learning design and content of their courses to cater to students' changing needs and provide more meaningful learning experiences.

AI and modes of learning

Integrating AI in higher education involves different ways and methods that affect learning, teaching, as well as administrative and management tasks; however, the main focus of this research is students' learning. Students learn through several learning modes available in higher education institutions; therefore, understanding how AI can be integrated with each mode of learning is essential to ensure that AI-based systems and tools are implemented and used in the most effective and efficient way. The education department of the government of New South Wales (NSW) in Australia has focused on researching the main learning modes utilised in higher education institutions. A detailed review of each mode is considered in the following sections in order to thoroughly understand them and ensure that the right AI tool or system can be integrated. The main learning modes described are collaboration, discussion, feedback and reflection, guided learning, explicit, demonstration, experiential, independent, and online (NSW Education, 2020; Xia & Zhou,

2021; Wang, 2022). The following description of the learning modes supports the collection of primary data to fulfil the gap in the existing literature, related to which AI tools are most relevant for each learning mode.

Collaboration

Collaboration is often defined as a philosophy of learning that involves sharing knowledge, experiences, and agency, with students learning from one another while developing positive interdependencies (NSW Education, 2020). Collaboration as a model of learning is considered to play a very important role in generating new ideas, solving problems, growing confidence, developing collective intelligence, and enhancing interpersonal skills. It involves a group of students working together where everyone contributes towards a common task to achieve shared goals. Drigas et al. (2023) suggest that in the future, employees with the ability to understand and assess the emotions of those around them and to adapt their behaviour accordingly will be the most sought after in the workplace. Hattie (2019) focuses the research on identifying several strategies for effective collaboration, such as cooperative learning, peer tutoring, positive peer influence, small-group learning, and the teacher–student relationship. Williamson et al. (2020) discuss that collaboration, as compared to competitive and individualistic work, benefits students for several reasons, such as greater productivity and higher achievement, better supported, committed, and caring relationships, improved self-esteem, social competence, and psychological health.

Discussion

Discussion is another mode of learning defined as an integral lesson component, taking place in a range of configurations such as whole-class, small-group, and pairs while occurring at any stage of the learning sequence with effective listening and speaking skills, to develop students' understanding of key concepts, empathy towards others, ability to reason, and/or capacity for critical thinking (NSW Education, 2020). Discussion is considered a meaningful dialogue where the dialogue is an educative process. Similarly, Budiyono et al. (2021) consider the discussion method as an activity where a number of people discuss together through an exchange of opinions on a topic or problem or seek answers to a problem based on all possible facts. Like collaboration, discussion incorporates a series of interpersonal skills as well as critical thinking. Hattie (2019) discusses some of the strategies related to this learning mode, including positive peer influences, questioning, elaborative interrogation, jigsaw method, inductive teaching, and classroom cohesion, etc. Furthermore, for a discussion to be carried out effectively, the following strategies should be followed: (1) The discussion should take place in groups with participants in it; (2) Opinions should be freely expressed by each participant; (3) The discussion process should be governed by mutually agreed rules; (4) The discussion should have a purpose to take place, and no pressure should be present from any of the participants; and (5) The discussion should be led by a leader who is able to keep the conversation to the point.

Feedback and reflection

Feedback and reflection are considered one learning mode; however, research demonstrates that they are two different concepts despite the fact that they have a lot in common in terms of procedures and results. Feedback is seen as a repetitive and recurring part of the education process, and it is both regular and immediate (NSW Education, 2020). Students are able to obtain feedback from their classroom friends, their teachers, and other physical and non-physical elements. The feedback can be manifested in different forms, such as writing, spoken dialogue, body language, etc. On the other hand, research on reflection shows that it relates to students focusing on self-analysis or self-examination to understand their learning experiences better at any stage of their learning (NSW Education, 2020). Hattie and Timperley (2007) state that feedback has a tremendously positive influence on learning, especially when it addresses three sets of questions: (1) Where am I going? / What are the objectives? (2) How am I going? / What has been achieved towards the set objectives?, and (3) What comes next? / What can be done to achieve better progress? Several conditions have been identified for successful feedback, including that feedback is valued by both learners and educators, learners are active in the process, educators judge effectiveness based on evidence, learners and educators have access to appropriate technology, learners know how to use the feedback provided, and feedback is tailored to learners' specific needs.

Guided learning

Guided learning refers to learning that takes place with some form of guidance, whether that is a competent, knowledgeable person or a technology-based system (NSW Education, 2020). Hattie (2019) argues that according to the Piagetian program developed by Piaget in 1973, the teachers are encouraged to know and understand the way students reason; how their reasoning can be constrained by their stage of development, and how to develop successive and simultaneous thinking. Further research concentrates on the fact that even though there is an increasing implementation of the technology, guided learning will remain relevant, as the need for guidance will always be present (NSW Education, 2020). Wang (2022) argues that guided learning focuses on teachers constructing student-learning protocols that comprise learning objectives, materials, methods, and procedures before the session and utilise them to guide students to engage in more autonomous learning. Benefits of guided learning include enhanced student classroom engagement (Xia & Zhou, 2021), improved teacher–student relationships and increased classroom learning efficiency (Wang, 2019).

Explicit (face-to-face learning)

Explicit learning mode is referred to as the explicit teaching of skills and content to students, often through carefully structured demonstrations, lectures, and presentations (NSW Education, 2020). It is mostly considered an old-style method suitable for large classrooms where knowledge and wisdom are shared by the teacher. Hattie (2019) focuses part of the research on pointing out some strategies related to explicit instruction, which comprise clear objectives by connecting goals to plans to overcome difficulties, utilising support to guide students during their learning process by ensuring that they have been clearly explained the purpose for learning the new skills and supported with feedback till independency is accomplished, clarity while explaining, providing examples and guided practice, and ensuring that the aims of the class and success criteria are clearly communicated. Further research demonstrates that explicit, face-to-face learning mode has certain advantages for students, such as real-time interaction between students and between students and teachers, enhanced motivation, building a sense of community (Singh et al., 2021), and the opportunity to seek clarifications for questions (Paul & Jefferson, 2019). On the other hand, Cooper (2022) argues that this type of learning mode has its own disadvantages, such as the lack of flexibility of learning at your own time and pace and students being uncomfortable with being surrounded by other students and talking in front of them.

Demonstration

Demonstration is the process of showing something, for example, ideas, concepts, processes, arguments, and visualisations, through reason and/or proof and clarifying with examples, experiments, and steps (NSW Education, 2020). Nihayatuzzahra (2020) argues that this mode of learning aims to help students seek and find answers to problems by completing their own experiments and enhances their scientific thinking. Similarly, Pangaribuan et al. (2022) discuss another benefit of the demonstration method, which motivates students to participate in learning, and instead of being passive, they contribute and are active throughout the lessons. Demonstration can occur in three different ways (teach demonstration, teacher–student demonstration, and student-group demonstration), and Akpan (2014) highlights three key factors for a successful demonstration mode of learning, including proper demonstration of the procedure to the students, the procedures being governed by safety precautions, and allowing time for students to absorb the knowledge, understand, and learn.

Experiential

Experiential learning is a mode of learning through the experience of *doing something*; it often incorporates other approaches such as cooperative learning, inquiry, field-based learning, and learner choice (NSW Education,

2020). This mode of learning is all about gaining knowledge practically; it ensures that students facilitate their learning and gain problem-solving skills. A teacher's role is usually considered as a guide who instructs students or models the necessary tools. Hattie (2019) discusses several strategies related to experiential learning, such as inquiry-based exploration, evidence-driven discovery, transfer of knowledge across contexts, tactile engagement, and the development of confidence, self-concept, and self-efficacy through reflection and feedback. Experiential learning is cyclical. The student gains the experience, reflects on it, forms new concepts and ideas based on the reflection, and uses what was learnt in new experiences. According to Gittings et al. (2020), several benefits have been identified related to experiential learning, including enhanced skills of understanding or retaining technical knowledge, increased student satisfaction, and increased ability to practically apply the theory.

Independent

Independent learning is an autonomous learning that is both a means and an end in education (NSW Education, 2020). According to Naibaho (2019), the independent learning mode is a learning strategy that aims to build individual initiative, independence, and self-improvement, strongly built by the students' learning motivation. Students who utilise this mode of learning can study independently, self-organise, self-regulate, independently find solutions for different problems, and make difficult decisions related to their learning. Even though independent learning is different from the other modes of learning mentioned earlier due to its independent nature, it is still closely related to them; for example, when a student studies or solves a problem individually but with the help of instructions from the teacher (NSW Education, 2020). Research completed by Hockings et al. (2017) demonstrates that when students study independently, they initially use low-level organising and reinforcing skills, and later on, they develop higher-level applying and extending skills. Furthermore, the authors suggest that successful independent learning is based on clear guidance, clear tasks, and support for students.

Online

According to Harasim (2000), online education became increasingly accessible in 1992 when the World Wide Web was invented. The first totally online course was introduced in 1982, and since then, it has continued to develop and spread across undergraduate, graduate, and executive education courses. The author argues that the online mode relies on networking as the primary teaching medium for an entire course or programme. Furthermore, Dhawan (2020) argues that online learning is defined as learning experiences in synchronous or asynchronous environments using different devices (e.g., mobile phones, laptops) with internet access. Similarly, Singh and Thurman (2019) highlight that online learning allows students to learn and interact with instructors and other students from any place and independently; however, students cannot receive instant feedback and immediate response. Course discussion and interaction take place through the use of the Web or computer networks.

The previously identified learning modes represent some of the most common ways students use to learn; therefore, they are all connected to AI and several tools and systems that are currently applied in higher education institutions. Considering the lack of data from secondary literature on which AI tools, platforms, or systems would be best suited for each of the above, they form the basis of primary data collection to understand the best AI technologies for each of the modes and the impact that these technologies have on students' learning. Kang (2021) argues that although the education sector has been impacted by innovation since the industrial age, usually innovation occurs at a slow pace; however, this has not been the case during the COVID-19 pandemic. The pandemic accelerated digital transformation in the education sector at a faster pace compared to previously. Similarly, Strielkowski (2020) argues that COVID-19 accelerated digital transformation in higher education and initiated novelties that would normally take years to happen, in just a couple of days, including changing the status of online learning from a disruptive process to a "messiah" status. This was made possible through the use of advanced technologies such as AI and ML. Shaikh et al. (2022) argue that AI technologies were used to fulfil the requirements of higher education during the pandemic and ensure that learning continued. The following section discusses AI and learning theories.

AI and learning theories

The increasing application of AI in higher education institutions impacts students and their learning in different ways, and it has its own benefits and pitfalls. Similarly, AI connects with learning theories and combines to create new paradigms. Chen et al. (2020), Hwang et al. (2020), and Hwang and Tu (2021) discuss the increased need for a close combination of educational and learning theories with AI technologies, given that this adoption would support learning and instruction. Based on the main learning theories, Ouyang and Jiao (2021) suggest that three AI education paradigms summarise how AI technologies are used to address educational issues: AI-directed (learner as recipient), AI-supported (learner as collaborator), and AI-empowered (learner as leader).

According to Xu and Ouyang (2022), paradigm one is focused on AI representing the key knowledge and directing the learning process for students, while they act as recipients of the services and follow specific pathways. The authors highlight that behaviourism is the theoretical underpinning of this paradigm. According to Reimann (2018), behaviourism is a psychology-grounded pedagogical line of thought, based on the idea that behaviour can be researched scientifically without consideration of cognitive states, and learning is influenced solely by physical variables such as environmental or material reinforcement. Behaviourists consider free will an illusion, and responses can be conditioned and determined. Given the characteristics of behaviourism learning theory, it aligns with the AI-directed paradigm where the learner is the recipient and has no choice in the learning path. Du Boulay (2019) discusses that in this paradigm, it is the AI system that defines the learning goals, content, and procedures, and only some systems collect information about the learners to understand their learning state.

According to Sachdeva (2022), paradigm two, or AI-supported and learner as collaborator, focuses on AI serving as a supporting tool for the learners. On the other hand, the learner acts as a collaborator with the system, and they build mutual and active interactions together to ensure a learner-centred personalised learning approach. According to Ouyang and Jiao (2021), cognitive and social constructivist learning theories are the theoretical underpinnings of this paradigm. Constructivism focuses on learners constructing their own meaning of the material and content provided to them in order to learn in the best way possible. Likewise, Rannikmäe et al. (2020) link social constructivism with a collaborative nature of learning and an important cultural and social context. Similar to social constructivism, cognitive learning focuses on learning that relies on both the internal thought process and the external factors like information or data (Fairbanks, 2021). Considering the nature of these two learning theories, their characteristics align with the AI-supported paradigm, given that learners act as collaborators, and they communicate with the AI systems to accomplish a more efficient learning experience (Baker et al., 2019). On the other hand, in contrast to paradigm one, the AI system collects individualised information for learners and uses it as an input to adapt the learning and provide an individualised learning experience (Rose et al., 2019).

The third paradigm, or AI-empowered, learner as a leader, considers AI as a tool to augment human intelligence, where the learner is the core of AI education (Law, 2019). In this paradigm, AI provides a high level of effectiveness, accuracy, and transparency and assists the learners to achieve augmented intelligence (Yang et al., 2021). On the other hand, the learners work as leaders of their own learning to achieve a better and more efficient learning experience by also focusing on managing the risk of the automated AI decisions (Gartner, 2019). Ouyang and Jiao (2021) argue that complexity learning theory is the theoretical underpinning of this paradigm due to its view of education as a complex adaptive system. Abaszadeh et al. (2019) highlight that complexity theory is characterised by six key features, including unpredictability, openness, dynamism, non-linearity, complexity and feedback, and adaptability sensitivity. Considering the complexity of this learning theory, its characteristics align with the third paradigm, which focuses on complex accomplishments such as the augmentation of human intelligence, capability, and potential. Furthermore, it focuses on enhancing the human–computer cooperation system, which integrates AI and human decision-making to achieve the learner-as-leader goal (Gartner, 2019; Law, 2019).

According to Ouyang and Jiao (2021), AI in education has moved from paradigm one, where the system directed the learner, to paradigm two, where the system and the learner collaborated, and it is currently moving towards the third paradigm, where the learner is the leader, and the systems adapt accordingly to assist the development of learner-centred learning.

Conclusion

AI has evolved from a theoretical construct into a practical and indispensable component of higher education. Its integration into universities has led to more dynamic, personalised, and data-driven learning experiences that complement traditional teaching methods. From Brain–Computer Interfaces and teacherbots to adaptive learning systems and intelligent feedback tools, AI continues to revolutionise how students and educators interact with knowledge. However, this transformation also requires thoughtful alignment with educational theories and ethical considerations to ensure that technology supports rather than supplants human creativity and judgement. Ultimately, AI represents both a challenge and an opportunity—one that, if harnessed responsibly, can enhance learning quality, foster innovation, and contribute to a more inclusive and future-ready academic landscape.

Reference list

Abaszadeh, S., Moinzadeh, A., & Eslami-Rasekh, A. (2019). Translator education in the light of complexity theory: A case of Iran's higher education system. *International Journal of Society, Culture & Language*, 7(2) Special Issue on Iranians Views of Cultural Issues, 52–68.

Accenture. (2022). *What is artificial intelligence (AI) & why is it important?* Accenture. [online] Retrieved October 22, 2025, from https://www.accenture.com/gb-en/insights/artificial-intelligence

Agnihotri, N. (2022). *What are different types of artificial intelligence?* [online] Engineers Garage. Retrieved October 22, 2025, from https://www.engineersgarage.com/what-are-different-types-of-artificial-intelligence/

Akpan, L. P. (2014). *Demographic variables and counselling effectiveness of secondary school counsellors in Akwa Ibom State, Nigeria* [Unpublished PhD Thesis]. Department of Educational Foundation, Guidance and Counselling, University of Uyo, Akwa Ibom State.

Aldosari, S. (2020). The future of higher education in the light of artificial intelligence transformations. *International Journal of Higher Education*, 9(3), 145–150.

Ali, A. M. (2025). Evaluating artificial intelligence readiness within faculty in the higher education sector. *Higher Education Quarterly*, 79(4), e70061.

Alimardani, M., & Hiraki, K. (2020). Passive brain-computer interfaces for enhanced human-robot interaction. *Frontiers in Robotics and AI*, 7, 125.

Alrakhawi, H. A., Jamiat, N. U. R. U. L. L. I. Z. A. M., & Abu-Naser, S. S. (2023). Intelligent tutoring systems in education: A systematic review of usage, tools, effects and evaluation. *Journal of Theoretical and Applied Information Technology, 101*(4), 1205–1226.

Avans University of Applied Sciences. (2022). *Avans University of applied sciences turns learning into an interactive experience using power virtual agents.* [online] Retrieved October 22, 2025, from https://customers.microsoft.com/en-gb/story/1523447657831033574-avans-higher-education-azure-en-netherlands

Badaró, S., Ibañez, L., & Agüero, M. (2013). Sistemas expertos: Fundamentos, metodologías y aplicaciones. *Ciencia y tecnología, 13*, 349–364. http://doi.org/10.18682/cyt.v1i13.122

Badillo, S., Banfai, B., Birzele, F. et al. (2020). An introduction to machine learning. *Clinical Pharmacology & Therapeutics*. https://doi.org/10.1002/cpt.1796.

Bai, H. (2022). Students' use of learning management system in hybrid learning: Mobile or not. In *International journal on E-learning* (pp. 5–23). Association for the Advancement of Computing in Education (AACE).

Baker, T., Smith, L., & Anissa, N. (2019). *Educ-AI-tion rebooted? Exploring the future of artificial intelligence in schools and colleges.* https://www.nesta.org.uk/report/education-rebooted/

Betz, S. (2022). *4 Types of artificial intelligence.* [online] Built In. Retrieved October 22, 2025, from https://builtin.com/artificial-intelligence/types-of-artificial-intelligence

Bircham International University. (2022). *NLP neuro linguistic programming.* [online] Retrieved October 22, 2025, from https://www.bircham.edu/nlp-neuro-linguistic-programming.html

Budiyono, S., Harta, D., & Yuliantoro, A. (2021). The application of discussion method for improving students' logical thinking skills. *Journal of Applied Studies in Language, 5*(1), 56–66. http://doi.org/10.31940/jasl.v5i1.2345.

Cameron, B. (2021). *Intelligent tutoring systems: Connection AI and education.* [online] Retrieved October 22, 2025, from https://crowdmark.com/blog/intelligent-tutoring-systems-connecting-ai-and-education/

Cao, J., Yang, T., Lai, I., & Wu, J. (2021). Student acceptance of intelligent tutoring systems during COVID-19: The effect of political influence. *The International Journal of Electrical Engineering & Education, 1*(1).

Chan, C. K. Y., & Tsi, L. H. (2023). *The AI revolution in education: Will AI replace or assist teachers in higher education?* ArXiv Preprint arXiv:2305.01185

Chen, X., Xie, H., & Hwang, G. J. (2020). A multi-perspective study on artificial intelligence in education: Grants, conferences, journals, software tools, institutions, and researchers. *Computers & Education: Artificial Intelligence, 1*, Article 100005.

Cooper, N. (2022). *Distance learning vs face-to-face—Benefits and drawbacks.* [online] Latest News. Retrieved October 22, 2025, from https://www.ncchomelearning.co.uk/blog/distance-learning-vs-face-to-face-benefits-and-drawbacks/

Crawford, K. (2021). *Atlas of AI* (pp. 7–8). Yale University Press.

Deng, L. (2018). Artificial intelligence in the rising wave of deep learning: The historical path and future outlook [perspectives]. *IEEE Signal Processing Magazine, 35*(1), 180–177. https://doi.org/10.1109/msp.2017.2762725.

Desire2Learn. (2022). *Higher education: Customer success stories.* [online] Retrieved October 22, 2025, from https://www.d2l.com/en-eu/higher-education/customers/

Dhawan, S. (2020). Online learning: A panacea in the time of COVID-19 crisis. *Journal of Educational Technology Systems, 49*(1), 5–22.

Dick, S. (2019). Artificial intelligence. *Harvard Data Science Review, MIT Press—Journals, 1*(1). https://doi.org/10.1162/99608f92.92fe150c

Drigas, A., Papanastasiou, G., & Skianis, C. (2023). The school of the future: The role of digital technologies, metacognition and emotional intelligence. *International Journal of Emerging Technologies in Learning* (Online), *18*(9), 65.

Du Boulay, B. (2019). Escape from the Skinner Box: The case for contemporary intelligent learning environments. *British Journal of Educational Technology, 50*(6), 2902–2919.

Eschker, S. J., & Liu, C. (2024). *Towards strong AI: Transformational beliefs and scientific creativity*. arXiv. https://arxiv.org/abs/2412.19938
Fairbanks, B. (2021). *5 educational learning theories and how to apply them*. [online] Retrieved October 23, 2025, from https://www.phoenix.edu/blog/educational-learning-theories.html?_tt=b8f22a3e-d9be-462d-a91d-2a6a7b174a2b
Felt, U., & Irwin, A. (2024). *Elgar encyclopedia of science and technology studies*. Edward Elgar Publishing.
Gartner. (2019). *Hype cycle for emerging technologies*. https://www.gartner.com/en/documents/3956015/hype-cycle-for-emerging-technologies–2019
Giannakos, M., Azevedo, R., Brusilovsky, P., Cukurova, M., Dimitriadis, Y., Hernandez-Leo, D., Järvelä, S., Mavrikis, M., & Rienties, B. (2024). The promise and challenges of generative AI in education. *Behaviour & Information Technology*, 1–27. https://doi.org/10.1080/0144929X.2024.2394886
Gittings, L., Taplin, R., & Kerr, R. (2020). Experiential learning activities in university accounting education: A systematic literature review. *Journal of Accounting Education*, *52*, 100680.
Goenka, N., Choudhury, T., & Ahuja, N.J. (2021). Enhancing Number Sense of Dyscalculia Learners by Pedagogical Agents: A Review. In: Hassanien, A.E., Bhattacharyya, S., Chakrabati, S., Bhattacharya, A., Dutta, S. (Eds.), *Emerging Technologies in Data Mining and Information Security*. Advances in Intelligent Systems and Computing, vol. 1286. Springer, Singapore. https://doi.org/10.1007/978-981-15-9927-9_80
Gupta, R., Srivastava, D., Sahu, M., Tiwari, S., Ambasta, R. K., & Kumar, P. (2021). Artificial intelligence to deep learning: Machine intelligence approach for drug discovery. *Molecular Diversity*, *25*, 1315–1360. https://doi.org/10.1007/s11030-021-10217-3
Harasim, L. (2000). Shift happens: Online education as a new paradigm in learning. *The Internet and Higher Education*, *3*(1–2), 41–61.
Harkut, D., & Kasat, I. (2019). *Introductory Chapter: Artificial Intelligence—Challenges and Applications*. Artificial Intelligence—Scope and Limitations. IntechOpen. Available at: http://dx.doi.org/10.5772/intechopen.84624
Hattie, J. (2019). *Visible Learningplus 250+ influences on student achievement*. Corwin. https://visible-learning.org/wp-content/uploads/2018/03/VLPLUS-252-Influences-Hattie-ranking-DEC–2017.pdf
Hattie, J., & Timperley, H. (2007). The power of feedback. *Review of Educational Research*, 77(1), 86. https://doi.org/10.3102/003465430298487
Hoboken, N. (2020). Pearson acquires interactive learning technology from smart sparrow. [online] *Prnewswire.com*. Retrieved October 23, 2025, from https://www.prnewswire.com/news-releases/pearson-acquires-interactive-learning-technology-from-smart-sparrow–300987673.html
Hockings, C., Thomas, L., Ottaway, J., & Jones, R. (2017). Independent learning—what we do when you're not there. *Teaching in Higher Education*, *23*(2), 145–161.
Huang, B., Huan, Y., Xu, L., Zheng, L., & Zou, Z. (2019). Automated trading systems statistical and machine learning methods and hardware implementation: A survey. *Enterprise Information Systems*, *13*(1), 132–144.
Hwang, G. J., & Tu, Y. F. (2021). Roles and research trends of artificial intelligence in mathematics education: A bibliometric mapping analysis and systematic review. *Mathematics*. https://doi.org/10.3390/math9060584
Hwang, G. J., Xie, H., Wah, B. W., & Gašević, D. (2020). Vision, challenges, roles and research issues of artificial intelligence in education. *Computers & Education: Artificial Intelligence*, *1*, Article 100001. https://doi.org/10.1016/j.caeai.2020.100001
IDP. (2022). *3 Universities offering Neurolinguistic Programming courses abroad*. [online] Retrieved October 23, 2025, from https://www.hotcoursesabroad.com/

study/training-degrees/international/neurolinguistic-programming-courses/cgory/hb.42–4/sin/ct/programs.html

In, J. (2017). Introduction of a pilot study. *Korean Journal of Anesthesiology*, *70*(6), 601.

Jisc. (2022). *AI in tertiary education: A summary of the current state of play* (2nd ed.). Jisc.ac.uk

Johnson, J. (2020). 4 types of artificial intelligence. [online] *BMC Blogs*. Retrieved October 23, 2025, from https://www.bmc.com/blogs/artificial-intelligence-types/

Joshi, N. (2019). 7 types of artificial intelligence. *Forbes*. Retrieved October 23, 2025, from https://www.forbes.com/sites/cognitiveworld/2019/06/19/7-types-of-artificial-intelligence/?sh=17f75cb1233e

Kabudi, T., Pappas, I., & Olsen, D. (2021). AI-enabled adaptive learning systems: A systematic mapping of the literature. *Computers and Education: Artificial Intelligence*, *2*, 100017.

Kang, B. (2021). How the COVID-19 pandemic is reshaping the education service. *The Future of Service Post-COVID-19 Pandemic*, *1*, 15–36.

Lateef, Z. (2022). *What are the types of artificial intelligence? | Branches of AI |* Edureka. [online] Retrieved October 23, 2025, from https://www.edureka.co/blog/types-of-artificial-intelligence/

Law, N. W. Y. (2019). Human development and augmented intelligence. In *The 20th international conference on artificial intelligence in education (AIED 2019)*. Springer.

Limna, P., Jakwatanatham, S., Siripipattanakul, S., Kaewpuang, P., & Sriboonruang, P. (2022). A review of artificial intelligence (AI) in education during the digital era. *Advance Knowledge for Executives*, *1*(1), No. 3, 1–9.

Lin, C. C., Huang, A. Y., & Lu, O. H. (2023). Artificial intelligence in intelligent tutoring systems toward sustainable education: A systematic review. *Smart Learning Environments*, *10*(1), 41.

Lohr, S. (2021). What ever happened to IBM's Watson? [online] *Nytimes.com*. Retrieved October 23, 2025, from https://www.nytimes.com/2021/07/16/technology/what-happened-ibm-watson.html

Marr, B. (2021). *What are the four types of AI?* [online] Retrieved October 23, 2025, from https://bernardmarr.com/what-are-the-four-types-of-ai/

Marsland, S. (2014). *Machine learning, an algorithmic perspective* (2nd ed., pp. 4–5). Chapman and Hall/CRC.

Minsky, M. L., McCarthy, J., Rochester, N., & Shannon, C. E. (2006). A proposal for the Dartmouth summer research project on artificial intelligence. *AI Mag*azine, *27*, 12.

Nabiyev, V. V. (2010). *Yapay zeka: İnsan bilgisayar etkileşimi*. Seçkin Yayıncılık.

Naibaho, L. (2019). The effectiveness of independent learning method on students' speaking achievement at Christian University of Indonesia Jakarta. *Asian EFL Journal Research Articles*, *23*(6.3).

Neeharika, C. H., & Riyazuddin, Y. M. (2023). Artificial intelligence in children with special need education. In *2023 International conference on intelligent data communication technologies and internet of things (IDCIoT)* (pp. 519–523). IEEE.

Nihayatuzzahra, N. (2020). *Penerapan metode demonstrasi dalam meningkatkan minat belajar siswa pada mata pelajaran Fiqih di kelas III MI NW Badrussalam Sekarbela Tahun Pelajaran 2019/2020*. UIN Mataram.

Nil, G., & Aras, B. (2019). Artificial intelligence in education: Current insights and future perspectives. In *Handbook of Research on Learning in the Age of Transhumanism* (pp. 224–236). IGI Global.

Nilsson, N. J. (2014). *Principles of artificial intelligence*. Morgan Kaufmann.

NSW Education. (2020). *Learning modes*. [online] Retrieved October 23, 2025, from https://education.nsw.gov.au/teaching-and-learning/school-learning-environments-and-change/future-focused-learning-and-teaching/learning-modes

Ocaña-Fernandez, Y., Valenzuela-Fernandez, L., & GarroAburto, L. (2019). Artificial intelligence and its implications in higher education. *Propósitos y Representaciones*, 7(2), 536–568. http://doi.org/10.20511/pyr2019.v7n2.274

Ouyang, F., & Jiao, P. (2021). Artificial intelligence in education: The three paradigms. *Computers and Education: Artificial Intelligence*, 2, 100020. https://www.sciencedirect.com/science/article/pii/S2666920X2100014X

Oxford Learning College. (2022). *Accredited level 3 neuro-linguistic programming diploma*. [online] Retrieved October 23, 2025, from https://www.oxfordcollege.ac/product/accredited-level-3-neuro-linguistic-programming-diploma/

Pangaribuan, B., Purba, N., Siahaan, K., Sidabutar, E., Sihombing, V., Simamora, D., & Matondang, J. (2022). The implementation of demonstration method to increase learning outcome in natural science lessons. *Jurnal Obsesi: Jurnal Pendidikan Anak Usia Dini*, *6*(4), 3680–3692.

Pappas, I. O., & Giannakos, M. N. (2021). Rethinking learning design in IT education during a pandemic. *Frontiers in Education*, *6*, 652–856. https://doi.org/10.3389/feduc.2021.652856.

Park, D. M., Jeong, S. S., & Seo, Y. S. (2022). Systematic review on chatbot techniques and applications. *Journal of Information Processing Systems*, *18*(1).

Paul, J., & Jefferson, F. (2019). A comparative analysis of student performance in an online vs. face-to-face environmental science course from 2009 to 2016. *Frontiers in Computers Science*. https://doi.org/10.3389/fcomp.2019.00007.

Petterson, D. (2021). 4 main types of artificial intelligence: Explained. [online] *SearchEnterpriseAI*. Retrieved October 23, 2025, from https://www.techtarget.com/searchenterpriseai/tip/4-main-types-of-AI-explained

Pillai, R., Sivathanu, B., Metri, B., & Kaushik, N. (2024). Students' adoption of AI-based teacher-bots (T-bots) for learning in higher education. *Information Technology & People*, *37*(1), 328–355.

Popenici, S., & Kerr, S. (2017). Exploring the impact of artificial intelligence on teaching and learning in higher education. *Research and Practice in Technology Enhanced Learning*, *12*(1), 1–13.

Quinn, D., & Goldstraw-White, J. (2022). *Artificial intelligence and its applications in security*. G4S Academy.

Rannikmäe, M., Holbrook, J., & Soobard, R. (2020). Social constructivism—Jerome Bruner. In B. Akpan & T. J. Kennedy (Eds.), *Science education in theory and practice. Springer Texts in Education*. Springer. https://doi.org/10.1007/978-3-030-43620-9_18

Reimann, A. (2018). Behaviorist learning theory. In *The TESOL encyclopedia of English language teaching* (pp. 1–6). Wiley Online Library. Available at: https://doi.org/10.1002/9781118784235.eelt0155

Research Excellence Framework. (2014). *ASR: Commercial, societal and cultural benefits of new advanced speech recognition technology*. Case study: University of Sheffield. [online] Retrieved October 23, 2025, from https://impact.ref.ac.uk/casestudies/CaseStudy.aspx?Id=9442

Rose, C. P., McLaughlin, E. A., Liu, R., & Koedinger, K. R. (2019). Explanatory learner models: Why machine learning (alone) is not the answer. *British Journal of Educational Technology*, *50*(6), 2943–2958.

Rüfenacht, M. (2020). *The 4 waves of AI: Does the winner take it all*? [online] Parashift. Retrieved October 23, 2025, from https://parashift.io/en/the-4-waves-of-ai-does-the-winner-take-it-all/

Russell, S. J., & Norvig, P. (2010). *Artificial intelligence: A modern approach* (3rd ed.). Prentice-Hall.

Sachdeva, R. (2022). *Artificial intelligence in Indian education industry*. researchgate.net

Schiff, D. (2021). Out of the laboratory and into the classroom: The future of artificial intelligence in education. *AI & Society*, *36*, 331–348. https://doi.org/10.1007/s00146-020-01033-8

Shaikh, A. A., Kumar, A., Jani, K., Mitra, S., García-Tadeo, D. A., & Devarajan, A. (2022). The role of machine learning and artificial intelligence for making a digital classroom and its sustainable impact on education during Covid-19. *Materials Today: Proceedings*, *56*, 3211–3215.

Sheikh, H., Prins, C., & Schrijvers, E. (2023). Artificial intelligence: Definition and background. In *Mission AI: Research for policy*. Springer. https://doi.org/10.1007/978-3-031-21448-6_2

Sheth, A. P., & Thirunarayan, K. (2021). The duality of data and knowledge across the three waves of AI. *IT Professional*, *23*(3), 35–45. https://doi.org/10.1109/MITP.2021.3070985.

Singh, J., Steele, K., & Singh, L. (2021). Combining the best of online and face-to-face learning: Hybrid and blended learning approach for COVID-19, post vaccine, & post-pandemic world. *Journal of Educational Technology Systems*, *50*(2), 140–171. https://doi.org/10.1177/00472395211047865

Singh, V., & Thurman, A. (2019). How many ways can we define online learning? A systematic literature review of definitions of online learning (1988–2018). *American Journal of Distance Education*, *33*(4), 289–306.

Smart Sparrow. (2022). *About Smart Sparrow*. [online] Retrieved October 23, 2025, from https://www.smartsparrow.com/about/

Spice, B. (2020). *New AI enables teachers to rapidly develop intelligent tutoring systems—News—Carnegie Mellon University*. [online] Cmu.edu. Retrieved October 23, 2025, from https://www.cmu.edu/news/stories/archives/2020/may/intelligent-tutors.html

Strielkowski, W. (2020). COVID-19 pandemic and the digital revolution in academia and higher education. *Preprints*, 2020040290. http://doi.org/10.20944/preprints202004.0290.v1.

Strielkowski, W., Grebennikova, V., Lisovskiy, A., Rakhimova, G., & Vasileva, T. (2025). AI-driven adaptive learning for sustainable educational transformation. *Sustainable Development*, *33*(2), 1921–1947.

Tănăse, I., Voicu, B. C., Chivu, R.-G., & Grejdan, E. F. (2024). The use of the OpenAI GPT-3 AI technology for marketing content purposes. *Journal of Eastern Europe Research in Business & Economics*. https://doi.org/10.5171/2024.350288

Taye, M. M. (2023). Understanding of machine learning with deep learning: Architectures, workflow, applications and future directions. *Computers*, *12*(5), 91.

UCL. (2022). *UCL medical school: E-Learning guidance*. [online] Retrieved October 23, 2025, from https://www.ucl.ac.uk/medical-school/current-mbbs-students/e-learning-guidance

Wan, T. (2020). *Pearson bets on adaptive learning (Again) with $25M acquisition of Smart Sparrow*. [online] EdSurge. Retrieved October 23, 2025, from https://www.edsurge.com/news/2020-01-22-pearson-bets-on-adaptive-learning-again-with-25m-acquisition-of-smart-sparrow

Wang, J. (2022). Let students engage in real learning: An evaluation of protocol-guided learning. *Science Insights Education Frontiers*, *12*(1), 1691–1696.

Wang, P. (2019). *How AI chatbots and virtual assistants will transcend the current constructs of education*. Retrieved October 23, 2025, from https://medium.com/humansforai/how-ai-chatbots-and-virtual-assistants-will-transcend-the-current-constructs-of-education-3b4ce47a4bd6

Williamson, G. R., Plowright, H., Kane, A., Bunce, J., Clarke, D., & Jamison, C. (2020). Collaborative learning in practice: A systematic review and narrative synthesis of the research evidence in nurse Education. *Nurse Education in Practice*, *43*, 102706.

Wu, J., You, H., & Du, J. (2025). AI generations: From AI 1.0 to AI 4.0. *Frontiers in Artificial Intelligence*, *8*, 1585629.

Xia, J., & Zhou, L. (2021). *Integration of teaching and learning protocols: Teaching practice and theoretical exploration*. Shanghai Educational Publishing House.
Xu, L. D., Lu, Y., & Li, L. (2021). Embedding blockchain technology into IoT for security: A survey. *IEEE Internet Things J Early Access*. https://doi.org/10.1109/JIOT.2021.3060508
Xu, W., & Ouyang, F. (2022). A systematic review of AI role in the educational system based on a proposed conceptual framework. *Education and Information Technologies*, *27*, 4195–4223. https://doi.org/10.1007/s10639-021-10774-y.
Yadav, S. P., Gupta, A., Nascimento, C. D. S., de Albuquerque, V. H. C., Naruka, M. S., & Chauhan, S. S. (2023). Voice-based virtual-controlled intelligent personal assistants. In *2023 international conference on computational intelligence, communication technology and networking (CICTN)* (pp. 563–568). IEEE.
Yang, S. J., Ogata, H., Matsui, T., & Chen, N. S. (2021). Human-centered artificial intelligence in education: Seeing the invisible through the visible. *Computers & Education: Artificial Intelligence*, *2*, Article 100008.
Zaraki, A. (2020). *An excellent talk from DARPA on the three waves of artificial intelligence (AI)—The Contextual Adaptation is the right direction to go: Explainable AI*. [online] Cardiff University. Retrieved October 23, 2025, from https://blogs.cardiff.ac.uk/ai-robotics/an-excellent-talk-on-the-three-waves-of-artificial-intelligence-ai-the-contextual-adaptation-is-a-way-to-go-explainable-ai/
Zhang, C., & Lu, Y. (2021). Study on artificial intelligence: The state of the art and future prospects. *Journal of Industrial Information Integration*, *23*, 100–224.

3 Opportunities and challenges

The impact of AI on business postgraduate students

Introduction

AI has emerged as one of the most transformative forces in higher education, particularly in postgraduate business programmes, where innovation and technology increasingly shape learning experiences. This chapter explores the dual nature of AI's influence—its potential to enhance and personalise learning and its accompanying challenges that affect accessibility, adaptability, and equity. By drawing on recent academic research and practical examples, the discussion analyses how AI-driven tools are reshaping teaching, learning, and assessment while simultaneously revealing the limitations and risks of overreliance on technology. Specific focus is placed on postgraduate business students, who represent a critical group navigating rapid digital transformation in both education and the workplace. The chapter begins by outlining the key challenges students face when engaging with AI-based learning systems, such as technological barriers, digital illiteracy, cost, and the risk of isolation. It then highlights the numerous benefits of AI for learning, including personalised education, improved feedback, collaboration, research enhancement, and the development of essential technological skills. Together, these themes provide a comprehensive understanding of how AI simultaneously disrupts and enriches postgraduate learning in higher education institutions.

Challenges of AI for business postgraduate students' learning

The application and exploitation of AI-based technologies in higher education is already a reality; however, AI is not (yet) ready to replace teachers but is presenting the real possibility to augment them (Haroud & Saqri, 2025). The changes that it is bringing to these institutions are and will continue to be profound; however, they do come with great challenges as well as opportunities. To date, literature covers some of the main challenges that AI technologies applied in higher education institutions possess for students' learning.

Superficial and limited technologies—Students utilise AI technologies available in the institutions where they study; however, it is important to highlight that these technologies and the services they offer to them only

DOI: 10.4324/9781003664161-3

provide superficial solutions and are limited for more complex endeavours of learning (Kabudi et al., 2021). AI technologies not only require an inordinate amount of data to operate, but they also do not necessarily understand what they are analysing (McCarthy, 2022). They can recognise patterns; however, they have a restricted ability to understand the significance of the patterns and interpret them. Solutions and services provided to assist students' learning through the use of AI technologies are useful; however, due to these systems being technology-centric and not human-centric, they lack emotions, feelings, interactions, etc. (Xin & Zhao, 2021). Communication, collaboration, problem identification, criticism, and risk identification (Yu, 2019) can be very limited, only based on what data algorithms have been created with; therefore, students' learning experience can be quite restricted and quite different from a usual human experience. For example, a teacherbot can explain a module to students; however, when it comes to answering specific questions, it can only do so if the information and data for that question have been added to the system. Ma and Siau (2018) state that the strength of AI is its speed, accuracy, and consistency. It is a lost cause to compete with AI on these dimensions. On the other hand, AI is still weak in soft skills such as creativity, innovation, critical thinking, problem-solving, socialising, leadership, empathy, collaboration, and communication. Singh et al. (2024) support the above arguments by stating that AI is quick and efficient, as it allows a multitude of tasks to be completed quicker and more efficiently; however, the author supports the arguments that AI also has its own weaknesses, mainly because it remains inhuman, cannot communicate emotionally, and can provide wrong solutions and responses at any time.

Lack of flexibility and adaptability—AI technologies developed and used in higher education institutions provide content and material for several courses; however, although they have been used for a couple of years, they still lack flexibility and adaptability (Owoc et al., 2021). Students differ from each other in terms of their interests, learning needs, and goals; therefore, with a lack of human interaction and reliance on AI technologies only, there is a need for more adaptability and flexibility in the learning content to fulfil those needs and provide more support. To date, this has not been fully achieved; therefore, many students could find it challenging to familiarise themselves with the material and content provided, make the most out of it, and achieve their goals. Kabudi et al. (2021) support the above by identifying that students consider AI systems as not adaptive to their needs, given that they focus on achieving technical objectives and ignore personal issues related to the learning process.

Cost—Another challenge for students that relates to the application and usage of AI technologies in the institutions where they study is the cost. These technologies are developing at a very fast pace; however, the cost of this development is quite high due to different factors such as the availability and format of data, the large amount of data needed, and the infrastructure required to build an AI system or platform (Carrico, 2019). Due to the high costs, universities may increase the fees for students until a low-cost AI is achieved (Dhawan, 2021). This could become not only a challenge for students' learning but also one of the reasons not to pursue a university degree, for both home students in the UK and international students. Mulling (2021) also argues that it will be costly for universities to deploy AI and invest in innovative technologies; on the other hand, in the long term, higher education institutions will experience cost-cutting benefits from AI. Similarly, Dilmegani (2022) suggests that AI models and platforms are expensive to build; however, they are cheap to run afterwards.

Digital illiteracy—Another major issue that impacts students' learning due to AI is digital illiteracy. AI has developed very rapidly in the last few decades; however, not everyone has access to it or can understand and use it. First, AI technology requires access to the internet to be applied and used. According to Johnson (2020), in the UK, 4% of the population live without penetration to internet access in 2020; however, it varies for different regions. In 2020, North America and Northern Europe were the two regions with the highest penetration rate (95%); however, there are still regions with very low rates, such as Middle Africa with only 12% (Johnson, 2020). Moreover, according to research conducted by the Annual Status of Education Report (Rural) 2018, in 596 government schools in India, access to computers in schools is restricted to only 21.3% of the students (Dhawan, 2021). Students who are less aware of technology and lack access find it hard to use and adjust to AI systems, and it is certainly worrying, considering that these systems are becoming a reality in the institutions where they are studying. Many researchers have focused on the above issues and classified some of the challenges into five categories: technological literacy and competency challenges, technological sufficiency challenges, technological complexity challenges, students' self-regulation challenges, and students' isolation challenges (Rasheed et al., 2020).

Technological literacy and competency challenges—Some of the challenges that are related to technological literacy and competency include: challenges in handling different user interfaces, and resistance to technology. More challenges have been highlighted in this category, including the challenge of learning new technology, lack of technological competency, intimidation by learning new technology, confusion, and resistance to looking for appropriate help online, and difficulty understanding directions and expectations while using AI systems (Nyathi & Joseph, 2024).

Technological sufficiency challenges and technological complexity challenges—Technological sufficiency and complexity challenges are mostly related to a lack of access to technology, technology distributed and accessed unequally, a lack of internet access, bandwidth that is too low, slow processing speeds, technical difficulties, and distraction as a result of very complex AI technology (Getenet et al., 2024).

Students' self-regulation and isolation challenges—Conversely, it is not only AI technology that leads to challenges for students' learning; students themselves may also encounter different problems, such as self-regulation and isolation. The application of AI technologies and systems has made learning more independent, which means that students need to manage their time and organise their learning without being told what and when to do it. This can easily lead to procrastination due to the lack of self-regulation skills (Lai, 2024). Lack of self-regulation skills is a challenge for many students, as a result of which there is less preparation before class, poor time management skills, and a lack of knowledge on how to request help online. Another challenge caused due to the high level of independence that AI systems bring is also students' isolation. A simple example to understand this challenge is online learning. When students utilise different AI systems to study online, whether that is with a human instructor or a virtual assistant, they may feel isolated and disinterested, as well as uncomfortable being the centre of attention (Bylieva et al., 2021).

Limited work has been completed to minimise the impact that digital illiteracy and technological challenges have on students and their learning; nevertheless, the draft report issued by UNESCO (2018) shows that changes will be implemented, and strategies and plans are being put in place. Examples include:

—The Sustainable Development Goals (SDGs) aim to ensure that all youth and a substantial proportion of adults achieve literacy and numeracy by 2030.
—The Broadband Commission for Sustainable Development aims that 60% of youth and adults should achieve a minimum level of proficiency in sustainable digital skills by 2025.

This shows that working towards a higher level of literacy and digital skills and access is a work in progress and requires a few decades of planning, strategies, and implementation to tackle the issues.

Benefits of AI for postgraduate business students' learning

Having considered the negative impact of AI on students' learning in the previous paragraphs, the following section covers a summary of the benefits and positive impact that AI has on students' learning.

Grading process—Owoc et al. (2021) state that students benefit from AI systems implemented to help with their exams and assignments grading process, as they receive quicker response and quicker feedback on their results, as well as personalised recommendations based on processing and analysing their answers. Second, certain AI applications can keep track of students' learning and remind them about different tasks. An example of this involves the Polish inventor, Peter Wozniak, and his application SuperMemo. The app, which functions because of spaced repetition, can keep track of what students are learning and when they are doing it. The app can recognise when the student is about to forget certain knowledge because it has not been revised for a certain period, and therefore it reminds them and recommends revision (Owoc et al., 2021). Other AI applications assist students by reminding them about important dates, as well as incomplete tasks. The chatbot called Pounce, which is used at Georgia State University, reminds students by text regarding incomplete tasks.

Evaluation and feedback—Furthermore, several AI technologies that utilise ML and natural language processing techniques help students receive evaluations and feedback for different matters while they are studying. Owoc et al. (2021) provide an example of a chatbot that collects opinions via a dialogue interface like a human interviewer; however, in this case, the user is required to do a lot less work than normally, and the chatbot can adapt each conversation to students' personalities and the provided answers. Yixue Squirrel Artificial Intelligence system can collect and analyse data related to students' behaviour and provide timely individualised feedback. By 2019, Squirrel AI was used in 2,748 colleges in China (Squirrel AI, 2022).

Speed—Another advantage of AI for students' learning is the speed of receiving responses. The IBM Watson cognitive computing technology has introduced chat functions that are able to answer these questions. 1,600 questions is the weekly average that students at Deakin University in Australia have asked IBM Watson to learn about the campus, as well as studying in the cloud. Owoc et al. (2021) state that Watson has answered more than 55,000 questions from students within 12 months of its implementation. Similarly, Dilmegani (2022) argues that AI machines enable faster processes, complete tasks faster, and are available 24/7. Furthermore, Pedamkar (2022) suggests that given that AI machines are not humans and can work 24/7, with no breaks and no limited hours, they can perform at a higher speed compared to humans, irrespective of season, timings, etc.

Technological skills—AI benefits students by developing their technological skills, which becomes vital for their learning since technology is part of everyday life, including the environment where people study and the future environment where students will be working. Using AI technology within their universities not only helps students with their learning but also familiarises them with the technologies and gains knowledge that can be applied in their future work environment (Dhawan, 2021). Just exposing students to AI technology is not enough to learn all the skills. As a result, due to the development of AI, students are now provided with an AI-driven tool developed by Coursera that helps to find what skills students lack and suggest the right courses for them to enhance those skills.

Collaborative learning—AI technological development has made a great contribution to students' collaborative learning, and it is redefining it on a scale that was not possible before, with systems and tools that connect students all around the world without the need to be physically in the same class or speak the same language (Dhawan, 2021). Examples include the application of different virtual assistants who not only assist with teaching but also consider the mental well-being of students and real-time conversation services. Goel (2020) argues that Watson's virtual assistants were considered one of the most transformative educational technologies over the last 50 years by *The Chronicle of Higher Education*. They assist collaborative learning because they can provide continuous experience to students and also offer tailored knowledge at any time, whenever it is requested by the students. Furthermore, AI can break geographical barriers and connect students who do not speak the same language or have disabilities with a simple tool, which is called Microsoft's Conversation Transaction Service. This tool aids the identification of speakers and transcribes the conversation in real time, and helps those who speak other languages or those who have visual or hearing deficiencies (Microsoft Corporation, 2025). Another example of this is the Presentation Translator, a tool that can be used for PowerPoint, which generates subtitles simultaneously word by word as per the speaker's talk, thus aiding students with language barrier issues and assisting their learning (Microsoft, 2022).

Mental well-being—Furthermore, AI chatbots are able to help students manage their mental well-being. This is an issue that highly concerns universities; yet sometimes they are stretched to capacity and students must wait longer than they should to be provided with counselling services (Rouhiainen, 2019). Woebot is a chatbot designed to help students better understand their own emotions with intelligent mood tracking. It leads to reduced waiting times and provides students with the necessary services at the right time.

Lifelong connections—AI is a technology that not only helps students learn while at the university and connect but also maintains those relationships in the future and continues learning and receiving support afterwards. Dhawan (2021) describes it as lifelong connections that can be achieved through an AI-based system that utilises an automated engagement platform, which can collect all the information for the alumni and provide different understandings and stories to keep them all attracted and increase their outreach. The technology helps in retaining the relationships through curating alumni's interests and providing them with personalised information. A well-structured alumni collaboration and connection can help the management of all alumni activities within the university. Anthony (2020) also argues that AI technologies help the creation of large databases of alumni and the facilitation, dissemination, and management of important information among different stakeholders of higher education institutions.

Contribution to research—Another great advantage of AI for students' learning is its contribution to research. Universities have many postgraduate researchers who complete their theses through extensive research and can take advantage of these technologies. Dhawan (2021) considers the opportunities of AI in research as exceptional, as it aids researchers to tackle complex issues, conduct experiments, and generate hypotheses. More specifically, AI assists them with technologies such as reference trackers, plagiarism checkers, fabricated data identifiers, etc., as well as processing very large amounts of structured and unstructured data. Another issue in research that AI can tackle is finding the right information. The amount of data available online is huge; therefore, securing reliable and relevant research material is crucial for any researcher. AI tools can assist in simplifying the above and help researchers reduce their research time and find relevant data (Bolaños et al., 2024). Moreover, AI tools and services such as chatbots, virtual assistants, speech recognition, language skills, etc., help researchers create surveys, evaluate them, and conduct interviews (Barari et al., 2025).

Personalised learning—AI technologies in education have a further positive impact on students' learning due to the ability to facilitate personalised learning. This concept has been researched by many authors who focused their research on AI in education, and it can be related to similar terms used, such as individualised learning, differentiated, and adapted learning, etc. Bai and Wang (2025) argue that due to the recent advancement of AI technology, the interest of higher education in it is increasing, given the increase in demand for flexible, customised, and self-directed learning. Khor and Mutthulakshmi (2024) define personalised learning as an educational strategy that adjusts pace, content, and instruction based on each student's particular needs, interests, and aptitude. Universities have many international students, with different cultures and backgrounds and diverse levels of knowledge and skills, such as speed of learning, absorption of information, etc. (Dhawan, 2021). Traditional learning focuses more on the "one size fits all" approach, where the differences amongst students cannot be considered; therefore, AI attempts to resolve this problem by providing an on-demand, customised learning experience (Al-Badi et al., 2022). There are many AI-driven applications and tools, chatbots, and virtual agents created to assist students with personalised learning. AI is even concerned with students' emotions to make the experience as personal as possible. Assuncao et al. (2022) argue that Emotion Artificial Intelligence, also known as Artificial Emotional Intelligence, is an advanced step in the AI growth to support personalised learning and is defined as the technology that enables systems to study non-verbal hints like countenance, body language, gestures, voice tone, and modulations to detect, analyse, process, and respond to the cues—such as anger, fear, happiness, sadness, shame, and surprise (Dhawan, 2021). It is used to make sure that students can effectively learn and absorb the information, and understand how engaged they are. Furthermore, Palanisamy et al. (2021) discuss that to ensure personalised learning is provided for students, learners' data is continually fed into the systems supported by assessment and real-time feedback.

Conclusion

The integration of AI into higher education presents both remarkable opportunities and complex challenges for postgraduate business students. On one hand, AI technologies enhance efficiency, provide personalised learning experiences, and foster collaboration across geographical and linguistic boundaries. They support continuous feedback, self-paced study, and improved research capabilities, equipping students with digital skills vital for future careers. On the other hand, the challenges associated with AI—such as high implementation costs, limited adaptability, digital illiteracy, and emotional detachment—highlight the importance of maintaining a balanced, human-centred approach to technological adoption. While AI can augment educators and transform learning processes, it cannot replace the empathy, creativity, and critical thinking that define effective teaching and learning. Ultimately, the successful use of AI in postgraduate education depends on thoughtful implementation, institutional support, and digital inclusion strategies that ensure all learners benefit equitably from its potential.

Reference list

Al-Badi, A., Khan, A., & Alotaibi, E. (2022). Perceptions of learners and instructors towards artificial intelligence in personalised learning. *Procedia Computer Science*, *201*, C, 445–451.

Anthony, B. (2020). Information flow analysis of a knowledge mapping-based system for university alumni collaboration: A practical approach. *Journal of the Knowledge Economy*, *12*(2), 756–787.

Assuncao, G., Patrao, B., Castelo-Branco, M., & Menezes, P. (2022). An overview of emotion in artificial intelligence. *IEEE Transactions on Artificial Intelligence*, *3*(6), 867–886.

Bai, Y., & Wang, S. (2025). Impact of generative AI interaction and output quality on university students' learning outcomes: A technology-mediated and motivation-driven approach. *Scientific Reports*, *15*, 24054. https://doi.org/10.1038/s41598-025-08697-6

Barari, S., Angbazo, J., Wang, N., Christian, L. M., Dean, E., Slowinski, Z., & Sepulvado, B. (2025). *AI-assisted conversational interviewing: Effects on data quality and user experience*. arXiv preprint arXiv:2504.13908

Bolaños, F., Salatino, A., Osborne, F. et al. (2024). Artificial intelligence for literature reviews: Opportunities and challenges. *Artificial Intelligence Review*, *57*, 259. https://doi.org/10.1007/s10462-024-10902-3

Bylieva, D., Hong, J.-C., Lobatyuk, V., & Nam, T. (2021). Self-regulation in E-learning environment. *Education Sciences*, *11*(12), 785. https://doi.org/10.3390/educsci11120785

Carrico, S. (2019). Good news: A successful AI project will cost 15 times more than you think. *Forbes*. [online] Retrieved October 30, 2025, from https://www.forbes.com/sites/forbestechcouncil/2019/07/02/good-news-a-successful-ai-project-will-cost-15-times-more-than-you-think/?sh=2389c9f2474d

Dhawan, S. (2021). *Artificial intelligence in higher education: Promises, perils, and perspective*. Expanding Knowledge Horizon. OJAS, *11*, 11–22.

Dilmegani, C. (2022). Advantages of AI according to top practitioners. *AIMultiple*. [online] Retrieved October 30, 2025, from https://research.aimultiple.com/advantages-of-ai/

Getenet, S., Cantle, R., Redmond, P., & Albion, P. (2024). Students' digital technology attitude, literacy, and self-efficacy and their effect on online learning engagement. *International Journal of Educational Technology in Higher Education*, *21*, 3. https://doi.org/10.1186/s41239-023-00437-y

Goel, A. (2020). *AI-powered learning: Making education accessible, affordable, and achievable*. arXiv preprint arXiv:2006.01908

Haroud, S., & Saqri, N. (2025). Generative AI in higher education: Teachers' and students' perspectives on support, replacement, and digital literacy. *Education Sciences*, *15*(4), 396. https://doi.org/10.3390/educsci15040396.

Johnson, J. (2020). Household internet penetration in the UK 1998–2020 | *Statista*. [online] Retrieved October 30, 2025, from https://www.statista.com/statistics/275999/household-internet-penetration-in-great-britain/

Kabudi, T., Pappas, I., & Olsen, D. (2021). AI-enabled adaptive learning systems: A systematic mapping of the literature. *Computers and Education: Artificial Intelligence*, *2*, 100017.

Khor, E. T., & Mutthulakshmi, K. (2024). A systematic review of the role of learning analytics in supporting personalized learning. *Education Sciences*, *14*(1), 51. https://doi.org/10.3390/educsci14010051.

Lai, J. W. (2024). Adapting self-regulated learning in an age of generative artificial intelligence chatbots. *Future Internet*, *16*(6), 218. https://doi.org/10.3390/fi16060218.

Ma, Y., & Siau, K. L. (2018). Artificial intelligence impacts on higher education. In *MWAIS 2018 Proceedings*, 42. AISel. Available at: https://aisel.aisnet.org/mwais2018/42

McCarthy, J. (2022). Artificial intelligence, logic, and formalising common sense. In *Machine learning and the city: Applications in architecture and urban design* (pp. 69–90). Wiley Online Library. Available at: https://doi.org/10.1002/9781119815075.ch6

Microsoft. (2022). *Presentation translator*. [online] Retrieved October 30, 2025, from https://www.microsoft.com/en-us/garage/wall-of-fame/presentation-translator/

Microsoft Corporation. (2025). *What is multi-device conversation?* Azure AI Services—Speech service. [online] Retrieved October 30, 2025, from https://learn.microsoft.com/en-us/azure/ai-services/speech-service/multi-device-conversation

Mulling, L. (2021). *Why universities need to digitalise, including AI, Blockchain, and Iot to survive*. [online] Retrieved October 13, 2025, from https://www.webinars4you.com/studyabroadblog/why-universities-need-to-digitalize-including-ai-blockchain-and-iot-to-survive/

Nyathi, T., & Joseph, R. M. (2024). Empowering South African educators: Navigating the challenges of digital teaching and learning competencies. *SA Journal of Human Resource Management/SA Tydskrif vir Menslikehulpbronbestuur*, *22*(0), a2591. https://doi.org/10.4102/sajhrm.v22i0.2591

Owoc, M., Sawicka, A., & Weichbroth, P. (2021). *Artificial intelligence technologies in education: Benefits, challenges, and strategies of implementation*. [online] Retrieved October 30, 2025, from http://www.ue.wroc.pl/en/

Palanisamy, P., Thilarajah, S., & Chen, Z. (2021). Providing equitable education through personalised adaptive learning and assessment. In *Back to the future—ASCILITE*. ASCILITE Publications, pp. 202–207.

Pedamkar, P. (2022). *Advantages of artificial intelligence | Top 7 most useful advantages of AI*. EDUCBA. [online] Retrieved October 30, 2025, from https://www.educba.com/advantages-of-artificial-intelligence/

Rasheed, R., Kamsin, A., & Abdullah, N. (2020). Challenges in the online component of blended learning: A systematic review. *Computers & Education*, *144*, 103701. https://doi.org/10.1016/j.compedu.2019.103701

Rouhiainen, L. (2019). How AI and Data could personalize higher education. *Harvard Business Review Education*. [online] Retrieved October 30, 2025, from https://hbr.org/2019/10/how-ai-and-data-couldpersonalize-higher-education

Singh, A., Saxena, R., & Saxena, S. (2024). The human touch in the age of artificial intelligence: A literature review on the interplay of emotional intelligence and AI. *Asian Journal of Current Research*, *9*(4), Available at: https://dx.doi.org/10.56557/ajocr/2024/v9i48860

Squirrel AI. (2022). *Our development and milestones*. [online] Retrieved October 30, 2025, from http://squirrelai.com/our-development-and-milestones

UNESCO. (2018). *UNESCO guidelines for digital inclusion for low-skilled and low-literate people*. Draft v1.2.

Xin, H., & Zhao, D. (2021). Trend of artificial intelligence aided industrial design. In *International Conference on Applied Human Factors and Ergonomics* (pp. 420–428). Springer.

Yu, S. (2019). *When artificial intelligence meets communications: The challenges we are facing | IEEE Communications Society*. [online] Comsoc.org. Retrieved October 30, 2025, from https://www.comsoc.org/publications/tcn/2019-nov/when-artificial-intelligence-meets-communications-challenges-we-are-facing

4 Ethical and regulatory considerations in AI-driven education

Introduction

The growing integration of AI within higher education has given rise to a complex set of ethical considerations that extend far beyond technological innovation. As universities increasingly rely on AI for teaching, assessment, and administration, concerns surrounding privacy, bias, transparency, accountability, and equitable access have become central to academic and institutional discourse. This chapter explores these ethical implications in depth, highlighting how they influence students' learning experiences, institutional practices, and policy development. Despite the rapid deployment of AI technologies across higher education, ethical research and regulatory guidance remain limited, leaving significant gaps in governance and accountability. In response, recent initiatives such as the Ethical Framework for AI in Education and UNESCO's AI competency frameworks have begun to address these issues by promoting human-centred and responsible AI use. Drawing on current literature and institutional developments, this chapter critically examines the most pressing ethical challenges—privacy, bias, fairness, security, accountability, transparency, and access—and assesses how universities and policymakers are responding to safeguard learners while maximising the educational benefits of AI.

Ethical concerns and institutional responses to AI in higher education

Ethical concerns brought on by the use of AI tools in higher education institutions are a major issue for which very limited research has been completed, and insufficient guidelines and policies have been created by institutions, organisations, and governments (Marín et al., 2025). Secondary data research from peer-reviewed journals, articles, books, news sites, and websites generated limited information on some of the ethical implications of AI for students and how they affect their learning; nevertheless, the data generated is incomplete. According to Kamali et al. (2024), existing scholarly literature examining the ethics of AI in education is relatively small in volume. Several

DOI: 10.4324/9781003664161-4

ethical questions arise as a consequence of using AI in higher education, and they relate to different groups and educational values, and how AI systems can change those values. Moreover, Akgun and Greenhow (2021) discuss that the ethical risks of AI in education certainly run counter to the presentation of algorithms as objective and value-neutral tools. Furthermore, according to Porayska-Pomsta et al. (2022), the application of AI in higher education raises widely applicable ethical implications for students and their learning.

The response from governments and institutions related to ethical implications has been very slow, with only a few recent developments to address these issues, even though they have only limited information due to the lack of research. General Data Protection Regulation (GDPR), introduced in the UK in 2018, only covers very limited questions related to the ethical implications of AI in education (Paddick, 2018). In 2018, the Institute for Ethical Artificial Intelligence in Education was created by Professor Rose Luckin, Priya Lakhani OBE, and Sir Anthony Seldon. They created the Ethical Framework for Artificial Intelligence in Education with the purpose of enabling learners to be protected from the risks AI brings while taking advantage of the benefits of this technology (Buckingham.ac.uk, 2021). The framework was updated in 2021; however, it does not guarantee the framework's fitness for purpose. A more recent development highlights UNESCO's launch of two new AI competency frameworks as part of the Digital Learning Week 2024. The first framework is aimed at students and the second at teachers, both aiming to address the specific nuances of AI. The frameworks stress a human-centred approach to AI education, promoting ethical considerations, responsible use of AI, and critical thinking (UNESCO, 2024). Both frameworks emphasise the importance of using AI responsibly by teachers and students, and the need to understand the potential and the risks that result from the use of AI. The frameworks provide a relevant roadmap for countries to develop AI strategies in education. However, a systematic review completed by Jodi et al. (2025) identifies that 85% of studies completed to date highlight that guidance on ethical AI in education is weak, and the need for standardised ethical frameworks is significant.

Key ethical and regulatory considerations and their impact on learning

Privacy

According to Stahl and Wright (2018), privacy is the biggest single focal point of ethics in AI. Alfredo et al. (2024) argue that AI can develop and improve only through adequate data access. Similarly, Im et al. (2024) state that to increase the efficacy and accuracy of AI, there is a need to give up some degree of data privacy. Currently, privacy issues within higher education institutions are regulated only through consent, which is considered a protective measure to collect personal data. Even so, the effectiveness of consent is considered doubtful. Lin Kyi et al. (2024) argue that informed consent is important; however, acknowledging multiple-page terms and conditions through a checkbox does not constitute true informed consent. With AI technologies developing and new features being introduced, privacy related to data collection could be a problem, as it needs constant reviewing and regulating. This may lead to these data being exposed and easily compromising security, privacy, and fairness, which then lead to ethical dilemmas (Dhawan, 2021). Raza (2021) argues that AI has empowered cybercriminals who intend to access sensitive information. Only in the first six months of 2020, 36 billion data worldwide were compromised. This is an example that data privacy is a major ethical issue, and the application of AI is only deteriorating the situation, given the large amount of data AI needs to operate.

Bias

Biases can be created and expressed by algorithms, and it is a natural feature of ML and human understanding (Mavrogiorgos et al., 2024). Professor Jan Willem de Graff (2019) states that data is always a limited reflection (measurement) of a limited part of reality. In essence, it is always biased. According to Li et al. (2023), biases can become an issue even without the intention of the creator of the model; therefore, students in higher education institutions may be subject to biases while using AI and experience several issues. AI tools are unable to explain why they make certain choices; planning and attentiveness are vital from the beginning, before harm is created. According to Katyal (2019) and Marinucci et al. (2023), there is a limited amount of work completed to understand implicit bias in human beings before we can more fully address how it works its way into AI. Examples of bias as an ethical implication of AI have occurred; however, there is limited evidence for higher education. An example of biases as a result of AI is the case of Amazon's AI recruiting tool, which showed bias against women. The system was trained to evaluate the Curriculum Vitae (CVs) based on the CVs submitted in the past 10 years. Given that most of the CVs submitted in the past were from male candidates, the system taught itself to favour males (Ravi, 2021). This is an example that shows that AI can lead to biased decisions, and this can occur in higher education institutions, especially if AI is used to accept or reject students' applications at the university.

Fairness and equity

AI systems that cannot be accessed by many and can be highly biased cannot be equitable (Bulathwela et al., 2024). Santry (2018) argues that disadvantaged school systems can become excessively dependent on AI by reducing human presence; given that AI proves effective and financially beneficial, however, the impact that this can have on students and their learning has not yet been considered. The author states that the risk of "school apartheid" is real if AI becomes available only to some learners and not everyone. According to Whittlestone et al. (2019), the technical accuracy of AI systems may run counter to what is fair or equal.

Security

Vulpe et al. (2024) argue that AI can assist the augmentation of cybersecurity; on the other hand, it can likewise assist the augmentation of efforts to bypass security. According to Dilmegani (2022), although existing measures have been legally implemented to protect sensitive data, further proactive measures are needed. Besides, further concern around security can lead to AI being targeted by actors with the intention of disruption and damaging an organisation's efforts and reputation (Tidjon & Khomh, 2022). An example of a potential breach of security occurred in Russia, when a Russian robot that was programmed to learn from the environment and interact with humans escaped to freedom from an open door in the facilities where it was kept (McDonald, 2017). If this occurs within higher education institutions and the AI-powered robot holds personal and sensitive students' information, there is a risk of breaching security and leaking data.

Accountability

Accountability is a crucial aspect of decision-making in AI, as AI-based interactions that prioritise diversity, inclusion, and fairness are designed to influence human behaviour, development, and learning (Faheem, 2024). Remian (2019) discusses accountability as an ethical implication of AI in terms of recognising failure, errors, and harm. The author argues that it is particularly easy to blame AI if errors occur and harm is caused, as people incorrectly believe that AI is autonomous and intelligent; however, it is worth understanding that AI is no more to blame than any other piece of software. Consequently, it leads to "deresponsibilisation" of developers and users alike (de Saint Laurent, 2018, p. 742). According to Allen et al. (2006), "an autonomous system that ignorantly causes harm might not be morally blameworthy, any more than a toaster that catches fire can itself be blamed" (p. 13); however, the inability to blame does not help the correction of errors, failure, or harm. Collina et al. (2023) argue that those who develop AI and those who decide to deploy it should be held responsible. The lack of accountability may expose students in higher education institutions to harm and leave them suffering the consequences with no options or corrections available.

Transparency

Transparency, as another ethical issue of AI, ensures that accountability can be found, and privacy is not at risk by focusing on understanding when and how AI is used (Cheong, 2024). According to Young (2023), the example of Jill Watson secretly acting as a teaching assistant brings up the issue of transparency of whether learners need to be informed of the fact that they are being taught by AI and not a human. The issue is around students' rights to know how their data is used, shared, and what predictions are made using their data. The author further discusses that students at the Maryland University College changed their opinion when they were better informed about how their data would be used. The General Data Protection Regulation, introduced in 2018 in the UK, states that the principle of transparency requires that any information addressed to the public or to the data subject be concise, easily accessible, and easy to understand, and that clear and plain language and, additionally, where appropriate, visualisation be used (European Union, 2016).

Access to technology

AI is currently used in higher education institutions and is generally accessed through online interfaces and computing devices; therefore, learners must have access to devices and the internet to be able to use AI in education (Hadar Shoval, 2025). Consequently, access to technology and devices becomes an ethical concern, taking into account that there are countries and higher education institutions where, due to socioeconomic factors, there is a lack of broadband infrastructure. The issue of accessibility becomes a problem for students who cannot access AI, as they miss out on education and the benefits of incorporating AI in education. Akmad and Abatayo (2024) state that studies have repeatedly demonstrated negative effects for learners in areas with no broadband or poor-quality access. Additionally, McElroy (2021) supports the fact that issues with access to technology and the internet lead to students not being able to demonstrate the same level of academic achievement as their peers. As universities shifted to online learning during the pandemic in 2020, the impact of the lack of accessibility to technology became even more obvious, given that more than one student out of ten does not have access to the internet or devices.

Conclusion

Ethical and regulatory considerations are at the heart of responsible AI integration in higher education. As this chapter has shown, while AI offers transformative opportunities to enhance learning and institutional efficiency, it also presents significant ethical challenges that cannot be overlooked. Issues such as privacy breaches, algorithmic bias, inequitable access, and a lack of accountability and transparency highlight the need for robust, standardised frameworks that ensure fairness, trust, and inclusivity. Institutional and global initiatives—including UNESCO's competency frameworks and the Ethical Framework for AI in Education—represent vital steps towards fostering a culture of ethical awareness and governance. However, continued research, cross-sector collaboration, and transparent policymaking are essential to address ongoing risks and ensure that AI remains a tool for empowerment rather than exclusion. Ultimately, the ethical future of AI in education depends on aligning technological progress with human values—upholding integrity, fairness, and respect for learners' rights at every stage of adoption.

Reference list

Akgun, S., & Greenhow, C. (2021). Artificial intelligence in education: Addressing ethical challenges in K-12 settings. *AI and Ethics*, *2*(3), 431–440.

Akmad, A., & Abatayo, A. V. (2024). Caught in the slow lane: Effects of unstable internet connectivity on accessing academic resources and collaborative learning. *Journal of Interdisciplinary Perspectives*, *2*(9), 278-286. https://doi.org/10.69569/jip.2024.0370

Alfredo, R., Echeverria, V., Jin, Y., Yan, L., Swiecki, Z., Gašević, D., & Martinez-Maldonado, R. (2024). Human-centred learning analytics and AI in education: A systematic literature review. *Computers and Education: Artificial Intelligence*, 6, 100215.

Allen, C., Wallach, W., & Smit, I. (2006). Why machine ethics? *IEEE Intelligent Systems*, *21*(4), 12–17. https://doi.org/10.1109/MIS.2006.83

Buckingham.ac.uk. (2021). *The institute for ethical AI in education | University of Buckingham*. [online] Retrieved October 30, 2025, from https://www.buckingham.ac.uk/research-the-institute-for-ethical-ai-in-education/

Bulathwela, S., Pérez-Ortiz, M., Holloway, C., Cukurova, M., & Shawe-Taylor, J. (2024). Artificial intelligence alone will not democratise education: On educational inequality, techno-solutionism and inclusive tools. *Sustainability*, *16*(2), 781. https://doi.org/10.3390/su16020781

Cheong, B. C. (2024). Transparency and accountability in AI systems: Safeguarding well-being in the age of algorithmic decision-making. *Frontiers in Human Dynamics*, *6*, 1421273. https://doi.org/10.3389/fhumd.2024.1421273

Collina, L., Sayyadi, M., &, M. (2023). Critical issues about A.I. accountability answered. *California Management Review*. Insight.

de Graff, W. (2019). Sorting machine. *Education Journal*, *378*, 18.

de Saint Laurent, C. (2018). In defence of machine learning: Debunking the myths of artificial intelligence. *Europe's Journal of Psychology*, *14*(4), 734–747. https://doi.org/10.5964/ejop.v14i4.1823

Dhawan, S. (2021). *Artificial intelligence in higher education: Promises, perils, and perspective*. Expanding Knowledge Horizon. OJAS, *11*, 11–22.

Dilmegani, C. (2022). *Advantages of AI according to top practitioners*. AIMultiple. Retrieved October 30, 2025, from https://research.aimultiple.com/advantages-of-ai/

European Union. (2016). General data protection regulation (GDPR)—regulation (EU) 2016/679. *Official Journal of the European Union, L 119*, 1–88. https://eur-lex.europa.eu/eli/reg/2016/679/oj

Faheem, M. A. (2024). Ethical AI: Addressing bias, fairness, and accountability in autonomous decision-making systems. *World Journal of Advanced Research and Reviews*, *23*(02), 1703-1711. https://doi.org/10.30574/wjarr.2024.23.2.2510

Hadar Shoval, D. (2025). Artificial intelligence in higher education: Bridging or widening the gap for diverse student populations? *Education Sciences*, *15*(5), 637. https://doi.org/10.3390/educsci15050637

Im, E., Kim, H., Lee, H., Jiang, X., & Kim, J. H. (2024). Exploring the tradeoff between data privacy and utility with a clinical data analysis use case. *BMC Medical Informatics and Decision Making*, *24*, 147. https://doi.org/10.1186/s12911-024-02545-9

Jodi, K. H. M., Zulfadli, M., Azizan, A. S. M., Husain, F. C., & Mohd Haridi, N. H. (2025). Ethical framework for artificial intelligence in professional practices of higher education lecturers: A systematic review. *International Journal of Education, Psychology and Counselling (IJEPC)*, *10*(57). https://doi.org/10.35631/IJEPC.1057013

Kamali, J., Alpat, M. F., & Bozkurt, A. (2024). AI ethics as a complex and multifaceted challenge: Decoding educators' AI ethics alignment through the lens of activity theory. *International Journal of Educational Technology in Higher Education*, *21*, 62. https://doi.org/10.1186/s41239-024-00496-9

Katyal, S. K. (2019). Private accountability in the age of artificial intelligence. *UCLA Law Review*, *66*, 54.

Li, M., Enkhtur, A., Yamamoto, B. A., Cheng, F., & Chen, L. (2023). *Potential societal biases of ChatGPT in higher education: A scoping review*. arXiv. https://arxiv.org/abs/2311.14381

Lin Kyi, K., Mhaidli, A., Santos, C., Roesner, F., & Biega, A. (2024). *"It doesn't tell me anything about how my data is used": User perceptions of data-collection purposes*. arXiv. https://arxiv.org/abs/2312.07348

Marín, Y. R., Caro, O. C., Rituay, A. M. C. et al. (2025). Ethical challenges associated with the use of artificial intelligence in university education. *Journal of Academic Ethics*, *23*, 2443–2467. https://doi.org/10.1007/s10805-025-09660-w

Marinucci, L., Mazzuca, C., & Gangemi, A. (2023). Exposing implicit biases and stereotypes in human and artificial intelligence: State of the art and challenges with a focus on gender. *AI & Society*, *38*, 747–761. https://doi.org/10.1007/s00146-022-01474-3

Mavrogiorgos, K., Kiourtis, A., Mavrogiorgou, A., Menychtas, A., & Kyriazis, D. (2024). Bias in machine learning: A literature review. *Applied Sciences*, *14*(19), 8860. https://doi.org/10.3390/app14198860

McDonald, G. (2017). *Ten alarming examples of AI gone wild*. [online] Retrieved September 30, 2025, from https://www.infoworld.com/article/3184205/danger-danger-10-alarming-examples-of-ai-gone-wild.html

McElroy, T. (2021). Addressing the digital divide in education: Technology and internet access for students in underserved communities. *Forbes*. https://www.forbes.com/councils/forbestechcouncil/2021/12/03/addressing-the-digital-divide-in-education-technology-and-internet-access-for-students-in-underserved-communities/

Paddick, R. (2018). *The ethics of Artificial Intelligence in education—University Business*. [online] University Business. Retrieved October 30, 2025, from https://universitybusiness.co.uk/news/the-ethics-of-artificial-intelligence-in-education-who-care/

Porayska-Pomsta, K., Holmes, W., Holstein, K., Sutherland, E., Baker, T., Shum, S. B., Santos, O. C., Rodrigo, M. T., Cukurova, M., Bittencourt, I. I., & Koedinger, K. R. (2022). Ethics of AI in education: Towards a community-wide framework. *International Journal of Artificial Intelligence in Education*, *32*, 504–526. https://doi.org/10.1007/s40593-021-00239-1

Ravi, R. (2021). *AI gone wrong: 5 Biggest AI failures of all time*. [online] Retrieved October 30, 2025, from https://www.jumpstartmag.com/ai-gone-wrong-5-biggest-ai-failures-of-all-time/

Raza, M. (2021). *AI cyberattacks and how they work, explained*. [online] Retrieved October 30, 2025, from https://www.bmc.com/blogs/artificial-intelligence-cyberattacks/

Remian, D. (2019). Augmenting Education: Ethical considerations for incorporating artificial intelligence in education. *Instructional Design Capstones Connection*. https://scholarworks.umb.edu/instruction_capstone/52.

Santry, C. (2018). Artificial intelligence 'risks school apartheid'. *Tes*. https://www.tes.com/news/artificial-intelligence-risks-school-apartheid

Stahl, B. C., & Wright, D. (2018). Ethics and privacy in AI and big data: Implementing responsible research and innovation. *IEEE Security & Privacy*, *16*(3), 26–33. https://doi.org/10.1109/MSP.2018.2701164

Tidjon, L. N., & Khomh, F. (2022). *Threat assessment in machine learning-based systems*. arXiv. https://arxiv.org/abs/2207.00091

UNESCO. (2024). *What you need to know about UNESCO's new AI competency frameworks for students and teachers*. [online] Retrieved October 20, 2025, from https://www.unesco.org/en/articles/what-you-need-know-about-unescos-new-ai-competency-frameworks-students-and-teachers

Vulpe, S. N., Rughiniş, R., Ţurcanu, D., & Rosner, D. (2024). AI and cybersecurity: A risk society perspective. *Frontiers in Computer Science*, *6*, 1462250.

Whittlestone, J., Nyrup, R., Alexandrova, A., & Cave, S. (2019). The role and limits of principles in AI ethics: Towards a focus on tensions. In *Paper presented at AAAI/ACM Conference on AI, Ethics, and Society*, Honolulu, HI, USA. https://doi.org/10.1145/3306618.3314289.

Young, J. R. (2023). *Georgia Tech is trying to keep a ChatGPT-powered teaching assistant from 'hallucinating'*. EdSurge. [online] Retrieved October 31, 2025, from https://www.edsurge.com/news/2023-06-22-georgia-tech-is-trying-to-keep-a-chatgpt-powered-teaching-assistant-from-hallucinating

5 Research design and methodology

A mixed-methods approach

Introduction

This chapter outlines the research design and methodology adopted to investigate the impact of AI on business postgraduate students' learning within UK higher education institutions. It explains the philosophical foundation underpinning the study—critical realism—and its suitability for exploring social phenomena that bridge human experience and technological advancement. The research employs a mixed-methods design, integrating qualitative data from semi-structured interviews and quantitative data from surveys conducted with MBA students and academics across multiple universities. This approach allows for both depth and breadth of understanding, combining statistical and thematic analyses to generate robust and triangulated findings. The chapter also discusses the inductive reasoning that guided theory development, the procedures used to ensure reliability, validity, and trustworthiness, and the ethical considerations that safeguarded the research process.

Research process

The review of the literature highlighted that research has been conducted related to the impact of AI in higher education institutions; this research mostly focuses on the benefits and challenges that AI brings for learners, educators, and the institutions themselves. Even so, the review also highlighted that there is insufficient research on how AI impacts business postgraduate students' learning, specifically in higher education institutions in the UK. Having considered this, the principal aim is to focus on the impact of AI on the learning of business postgraduate students, only in the higher education institutions in the UK. More specifically, the research focuses on critically examining the AI tools that can be identified for each learning mode, as well as the ethical implications arising from these tools and their impact on business postgraduate students' learning in higher education institutions in the UK. Twenty-four higher education institutions in the UK were considered, and samples were selected to complete the data collection process.

DOI: 10.4324/9781003664161-5

To address the concerns and insufficiencies identified in the exploratory literature review using secondary data, this research considered a mixed-method qualitative and quantitative design, within the critical realist approach, which has been chosen as the research philosophy for this research. Critical realism distinguishes between knowledge (epistemology) and existence (ontology). Hoddy (2019) argues that within critical realism, the world consists of natural and social objects, and the reality is stratified into three key domains: "the real" (natural and social objects), "the actual" (events), and "the empirical" (perceptions and experiences of events).

The research was divided into two main stages: the first being the exploratory stage and the second being the explanatory (descriptive) stage. During the first exploratory stage, secondary data collection was completed through a desk-based review of the literature to understand the research to date on the impact of AI on students' learning in higher education institutions. The second stage focused on accomplishing the aim and objectives and understanding the impact of AI on business postgraduate students' learning in higher education institutions in the UK, through the collection of primary data, gathered via semi-structured interviews and a survey. More specifically, the survey was sent out to MBA students in 22 universities in the UK and to MBA academics/professionals in these universities. Semi-structured interviews were conducted with MBA students and MBA academics/professionals within the Business Schools of six universities in the UK. Analysis of the interviews was completed through qualitative methods, and analysis of the survey was completed through quantitative methods. The ethical considerations of this research include the following: university approval, participants' informed consent, voluntary participation of the participants, anonymity and confidentiality of the data collected, storage, copyright, plagiarism, and use of the internet as a source to contact participants.

Research philosophy

Ogeyik and Uzun (2022) refer to the research philosophy as the philosophical perspective or stance that is decisive in determining the methodological assumptions of a research study. A credible research philosophy consists of well-thought-out and consistent set of assumptions. These assumptions include human knowledge (epistemological assumptions), reality (ontological assumptions), and the extent to which your own values influence the research process (axiological assumptions) (Abu-Alhaiya, 2019). It leads to well-supported choices of the methodology, research strategy, data collection, and data analysis. This provides a great opportunity to create a comprehensible and articulate research project, where all research elements fit together (Al-Ababneh, 2020).

Bell et al. (2022) state that each research philosophy provides a unique and valuable contribution to research; therefore, a deep understanding of each is needed to explore the differences and make the right choices in relation to each specific research. Considering the aim and objectives of this research, critical realism and interpretivism were considered by the researcher, as they focus on understanding and explaining human and social reality and seek explanations for social phenomena (Stutchbury, 2022).

According to Al-Ababneh (2020), critical realism focuses on explaining what we see and experience and understanding that what we see is not necessarily what we get; therefore, more criticism is required. Critical realism assumes judgemental rationality, which allows researchers to evaluate and compare the explanatory power of different theoretical explanations and, finally, to select theories that most accurately represent the domain of real given our existing knowledge. Furthermore, Stutchbury (2022) argues that critical realism is about searching for explanations (mechanisms), through focusing on what people can achieve (agency), in the social context they operate (structures). The author continues by stating that critical realism considers reality as an iceberg, where most of the iceberg, in this case, the reality, is unseen from the observer.

Critical realism combines both a realist ontology, which focuses on the fact that there is something to find out about, and a relativistic epistemology, which shows that different people know different things in different ways (Stutchbury, 2022). According to critical realists, the world can be understood through two steps: first, the sensations and events we experience, and second, understanding that after the experience, mental processing goes on, and we start reasoning backwards from the experience to the underlying reality that has caused them (Armstrong, 2019).

Interpretivism, as another research philosophy, was also considered; however, after consideration, it was not used for the purpose of this research. Interpretivism was developed as a critique of positivism, similar to critical realism, but from a subjective perspective (Alharahsheh & Pius, 2020). Interpretivists argue that physical phenomena are different from humans, because humans can create meanings that are then studied by interpretivists. Due to these differences, interpretivists argue that humans and the social world cannot be studied in the same way as physical phenomena (Alharahsheh & Pius, 2020). Al-Ababneh (2020) argues that interpretivism concentrates on generating interpretations of the social life world and developing knowledge by dealing with complicated situations in a subjective and descriptive method rather than a statistical and objective method.

Interpretivism is a very appropriate research philosophy for business and management research because situations or issues within different organisations and institutions can be very difficult and distinctive, based on many aspects such as context, time, circumstances, etc., and it is relevant in understanding humans and their social world. However, critical realism was considered the most appropriate research philosophy for several reasons. Critical realism offers a more epistemologically and ontologically grounded alternative for integrating qualitative and quantitative methods (Mukumbang, 2021); thus, it has been seen as more applicable given that this research focuses on a mixed-method approach. The research aims at exploring the impact of AI on business postgraduate students' learning in higher education institutions in the UK, which is a social phenomenon. Therefore, critical realism has been seen as appropriate given that it goes beyond the descriptions of interpretivism and seeks and generates rich explanations of the particular social phenomenon. Finally, the application of AI in different higher education institutions can vary based on what technologies they use and what areas of development they focus mostly. The research using critical realism focuses on the observable events and the unobservable structures and distinguishes between the real (development, application of AI and its tools), the actual (students' learning is changing), and the empirical (the impact of these changes on students' learning) (Stutchbury, 2022).

Trustworthiness in qualitative and quantitative research

This research focuses on the collection of qualitative data; however, it uses a mixed-method approach (qualitative and quantitative) to analyse the data in order to ensure triangulation of the findings and to ensure a better understanding of the phenomenon under study. Therefore, criteria to ensure trustworthiness of the research have been considered for both approaches (qualitative and quantitative).

Overall discussion on reliability and validity in qualitative and quantitative research

In the realm of research quality, the concepts of validity and reliability carry significant weight. These are recognised as the two most widely acknowledged quality standards applicable to both quantitative and qualitative research. Originating from the domain of quantitative research, which aligns with positivism and seeks to establish generalisable laws, the integration of these quality criteria into qualitative research can sometimes pose challenges (Vu, 2021). Silverman (2006, p. 282) explores the concept of reliability in quantitative research, defining it as "the degree to which an experiment, test, or measurement consistently produces the same result when repeated". This perspective aligns with the idea that reliability is linked to the "consistency of data, scores, or observations collected through research instruments" (Chalhoub-Deville, 2006, p. 2). These examples of defining reliability demonstrate that consistency is a shared characteristic of reliability. However, this approach sparks two significant debates: (1) what exactly constitutes consistency (reliability); and (2) the challenge of maintaining consistency within the subjectivist/constructivist epistemological framework that underpins qualitative research.

Silverman (2006, p. 283) dismisses the concept of reliability in qualitative research based on its epistemological stance. He argues that the positivist view of reliability assumes a static universe where research can logically be replicated. This assumption clashes with the qualitative/interpretive perspective, which maintains that the world is in constant flux, rendering the concept of replication problematic. Wolcott (2005) further elaborates on the characteristics of qualitative research, emphasising that consistency is ill-suited for the study of human behaviour in natural, unaltered settings. Consequently, offering reliability estimates for qualitative data is not a common practice, as many qualitative researchers concentrate on outlining methods to enhance the reliability of their approach. These debates have led qualitative researchers to reconsider their perspective on reliability. They believe that reliability should be in line with the theoretical foundations of their research. Some authors opt for different terminology, such as "dependability" instead of "reliability". Merriam (2009) recommends employing various techniques and involving multiple analysts to enhance dependability, including triangulation, peer review, the researcher's position, and maintaining a comprehensive audit trail.

Considering that this research focuses on qualitative data as one of the methods, reliability is a concept that has been considered carefully. In view of the difficulty of enhancing reliability in a qualitative approach, the research has employed two of the techniques suggested by Merriam (2009), triangulation and low-interference description. Triangulation involves the practice of cross-verifying data using multiple sources. Various forms of triangulation exist, including method, data, investigator, theory, and environmental triangulation (Burns, 2010; Merriam, 2009). Method triangulation, for instance, entails the use of diverse data collection methods, such as combining a questionnaire with subsequent interviews. This research adopted a method of triangulation, thus allowing triangulation of interviews with the survey and existing data in the literature. On the other hand, low-inference description demands that researchers present data in a comprehensive and specific manner without altering or reconstructing the information themselves (Silverman, 2006). This approach enables readers to critically assess the research findings. This technique was also employed for the qualitative analysis, by ensuring that the interview quotes from different participants were clearly highlighted and presented in the analysis to ensure that the researcher would not be able to alter their meaning.

Internal validity concerns the rigour of the research, while external validity is concerned with the ability to extend the findings beyond the studied sample. However, these definitions may not be particularly relevant for a qualitative researcher whose focus lies in comprehension rather than generalisation. In a broader context, validity is defined as a measure of truth (Nunan & Bailey, 2009). For instance, Vu (2021) argues that in the social sciences, validity serves as an epistemic criterion, signifying that research findings are accurate representations of the phenomena they address and are well-supported by evidence or justification. However, this definition faces resistance from qualitative researchers who hold varying views on truth. This rejection arises because defining validity as truth implies a rigid boundary between what is true and what is not, which contradicts the constructivist perspective acknowledging multiple truths. In response, qualitative researchers employ alternative validity concepts like trustworthiness, worthwhileness, or credibility, attainable through various specific strategies (Vu, 2021).

In quantitative research, the emphasis is on the consistency of findings, which can be replicated in diverse contexts, while qualitative research prioritises transparency and the ability to apply findings to other settings. In quantitative research, validity centres on the appropriateness of the research tool for the observed subject and the alignment of results with reality. In contrast, valid qualitative research requires evidence and trustworthiness. Because of these differences, qualitative research uses various terms to describe concepts like reliability and validity. These terms encompass credibility, dependability, trustworthiness, transparency, and transferability (Vu, 2021). In the following section, these crucial aspects are further explored in detail.

Discussion of criteria for qualitative research

This research outlines the criteria for qualitative research identified by Lincoln and Guba in 1985, which include credibility, dependability, transferability, and confirmability; however, a fifth criterion has been considered by researchers, authenticity (Kyngäs et al., 2020). Even though many researchers argue about what constitutes trustworthiness, many qualitative researchers have accepted these five criteria to ensure trustworthiness in qualitative research.

The first criterion considered for this research was credibility. This is the most important criterion because it provides confidence in the truth of the research. Credibility is concerned with understanding if the research findings represent a credible interpretation of the original data (Kyngäs et al., 2020). In this specific research, chapters 1 through 5 provide a true and clear picture of the phenomenon, specifically through secondary data. These data were collected through reliable sources such as peer-reviewed academic journals, online news articles, and blogs to understand the impact of AI in different aspects of higher education institutions, such as teaching, learning, and management/administration of these institutions. These sources of information aided the design of the survey and semi-structured interview.

Dependability is the second criterion considered for this research. Dependability refers to how stable the data are over time and over the conditions of the research. Shenton and Andrew (2004) argue that dependability is very difficult in qualitative research due to the changing conditions over time and the phenomena studied. However, this research clearly analyses the impact of AI on business postgraduate students' learning in higher education institutions in the UK. Moreover, the research provides detailed information about the interviewed participants, the methods used to select them, and the methods used to collect the data, to ensure that other researchers in the future can repeat the research in the same way to obtain similar findings.

The third criterion, transferability, relates to how useful the findings of a research are to persons in other settings and how applicable they are to different situations (Stumpfegger, 2017). This is also difficult in qualitative research since researchers do not generalise someone's story as everyone's. This research provides thorough information about the impact that AI has on higher education institutions in the UK. Furthermore, the research provides a detailed analysis of how the data have been collected and how they have been analysed. Considering the analysis and the findings, the results can be transferable to other higher education institutions within the UK and outside, as well as to similar institutions that have embraced AI technologies for their employees.

Conformability is the fourth criterion. According to Stahl and King (2020), conformability is the degree to which the results of the research can be repeated and are consistent and reflect the participants' opinions and experiences. In this research, the researcher ensured the criterion was met in two ways. First, a considerable amount of time was spent during and after the interviews to ensure the views of the participants were summarised correctly. Second, the interviews were transcribed, and the results were compared to each other and the survey. The survey results were analysed too and compared with each other, and all the data collected were triangulated to ensure accurate findings related to how AI impacts business postgraduate students' learning in higher education institutions in the UK. All the above steps ensured that the findings of the research resulted from the data set and not the researcher's predispositions. This allows the research to be repeated and to obtain consistent results, allowing increased levels of trustworthiness.

Finally, authenticity is concerned with the ability of researchers to accurately depict the diverse realities that exist in the data collected from participants (Kyngäs et al., 2020). This research ensures that the criterion has been met by including citations from all the participants and not only citations that reflect a single participant. Furthermore, all the citations used originate from the original data, and no changes have been made when using them. The researcher has ensured that no participants can be identified using citations. Finally, the researcher has ensured that the findings section does not include more citations than interpretations, and citations are not repeated more than once.

Discussion of criteria for quantitative research

In terms of trustworthiness of quantitative research, several criteria have been identified by researchers, including internal validity, external validity, reliability, and objectivity (Stumpfegger, 2017). Internal validity is the extent to which observed differences in the dependent variable are directly related to the independent variable, whereas external validity refers to how generalisable the results of the research are beyond the sample that is actually studied (Baldwin, 2018). Trochim (2006) identifies reliability as "consistency" or "repeatability", which is achieved if a measure provides the same results. On the other hand, objectivity is achieved when the researcher remains distant from the research completed and the findings do not depend on the values, personality, or the researcher's beliefs. For this research, external validity, reliability, and objectivity have been mainly considered, given that the data collected are qualitative but analysed using both quantitative and qualitative techniques. The research ensures external validity, given that the findings can be generalised throughout the UK higher education institutions and internationally if generalisability occurs with caution and the framework is adapted to specific institutions, learning modes, culture, and background in that particular country. External validity and reliability are also ensured through the process of triangulation of data. The research used both survey and semi-structured interviews to collect data, thus allowing for the triangulation of findings to occur. Furthermore, objectivity has been maintained, and the researcher has not implicated the findings with personal opinions, beliefs, or values. According to Noble and Heale (2019), triangulation of findings ensures that biases that may arise through the use of a single method or a single researcher are overcome. Considering the above, all the criteria of trustworthiness have been met, and allowed the researcher to understand the phenomenon and events within higher education institutions in the UK related to the impact of AI on students' learning.

Research approach

Choosing the right research approach for research is imperative as it guides the researchers throughout the process of theory development. Inductive and deductive approaches are the two broad methods in research. The inductive approach is used when there is a lack of theory or limited theory, or findings for a particular phenomenon. The approach allows for the emergence of new tentative hypotheses, which are first tested and then used to generate new theories and findings. The inductive approach allows theory to emerge from data, and the researcher should begin with an open mind and as less presumptions as possible. The inductive approach aims to generate meanings from the data set collected to identify patterns and relationships to build a theory; however, it does not prevent the researcher from using existing theory to formulate the research question to be explored (Corley et al., 2021). On the other hand, a deductive approach is concerned with developing hypotheses based on existing theory. Through deduction, after developing a hypothesis based on the theory, the empirical world can then be explored to test the truth or falsify the hypothesis. Lastly, the abductive approach is the use of both deductive and inductive approaches together, where the researcher moves from theory to data and from data to theory. According to Sharifah (2020), the abductive approach is useful compared to just using only one approach, inductive or deductive. Considering the aim of this research, which is to understand and critically examine the impact of AI on business postgraduate students' learning in higher education institutions in the UK, the inductive approach was deemed the most appropriate. The reason behind the choice was that the research aimed at generating findings that were limited in the existing theory, and the need for new hypotheses arose.

Research strategy

Qualitative and quantitative (mixed method)

Qualitative research can be conducted in natural settings, and it focuses on finding answers to questions (Hays & McKibben, 2021). It does not require firm regulations and guidelines, and it is used to collect information from participants to be able to identify themes and develop theories inductively. On the other hand, quantitative research focuses on cause-and-effect thinking, the use of measurement and observations, and the testing of the theories using experiments and surveys. The key difference between these two approaches lies in the distinction between explanation and understanding as the focus of exploration.

This research adopted a mixed-method approach focusing mainly on the qualitative research strategy due to the nature of the aim and objectives, as well as the inductive approach used; however, quantitative results were also generated and analysed using Statistical Package for Social Sciences (SPSS) to complete descriptive statistics and correlation analysis to allow comparison of the results and more efficient triangulation of data. The qualitative research strategy allowed the researchers to make sense of the social world within higher education institutions in the UK and understand the impact of AI on business postgraduate students' learning within these institutions. The quantitative approach stimulated the researcher's cause-and-effect thinking and generated statistical data through statistical analysis. A mixed-method approach presents numerous advantages for tackling complex research challenges by incorporating the philosophical foundations of post-positivism and interpretivism. It seamlessly blends qualitative and quantitative data to provide a comprehensive understanding of research issues. This methodology not only establishes a solid foundation but also allows for methodological flexibility and a profound comprehension of individual cases. In essence, the utilisation of mixed methods equips researchers to address research questions in both depth and breadth, facilitating the generalisation of findings and their relevance to broader populations. Another key rationale for combining these two approaches lies in the belief that each type of research holds intrinsic value, and, in certain respects, they complement each other. Consequently, there is added value in integrating them. Thematic analysis was used to analyse the interviews and generate the key themes, which led to the key qualitative findings of the research. On the other hand, descriptive statistics, correlation, and the Wilcoxon signed rank test are statistical analyses completed to analyse the findings from the survey.

Triangulation

Triangulation is a method that helps increase the validity, reliability, and legitimation, which encompasses credibility, dependability, confirmability, and transferability, of research findings (Renz et al., 2018). Due to the possibility of collecting data through different sources, triangulation also helps to validate the data collected. According to Bellido-Garcia et al. (2022), four types of triangulations have been identified: method triangulation, investigator triangulation, theory triangulation, and data source triangulation. This research utilised a mixed-method or method triangulation, which uses more than one research method, such as secondary data through existing literature, semi-structured interviews, and a survey to collect the data from the selected participants. According to Hays and McKibben (2021), the intent of the researcher is to learn from the participants and gather as much information as possible related to the specific phenomenon that is being studied. Using a mixed-method approach allows for more information to be collected and data to be validated, and generates different viewpoints related to the phenomenon studied.

The process of triangulation is crucial for establishing the validity and credibility of the research. Validity in research primarily addresses how accurately a particular approach measures something and how closely the findings align with the actual values or concepts under investigation. It signifies whether the findings can be trusted and correctly used, allowing stakeholders to make informed and appropriate decisions based on the research outcomes. Validity also plays a critical role in ensuring that the findings can be generalised to other geographical areas, populations, settings, conditions, and timeframes. Internal validity is essential for eliminating potential biases that might hinder research findings. External validity can be categorised as population validity, ensuring that the sample is representative of the studied population, and ensuring that findings can be applied across different contexts and time periods. The research employed triangulation to enhance validity and credibility while researching the impact of AI on students' learning in higher education institutions in the UK.

The key advantage of triangulation for the research is its role in confirming research findings. When researchers utilise various methods, such as both quantitative and qualitative methods, and all these methods consistently point towards a specific outcome, the results are effectively confirmed. This confirmation validates the accuracy of the work. Second, when a researcher employs a variety of methods, the weaknesses of one method can be offset by the strengths of another. For example, in this research, when both quantitative and qualitative methods are concurrently used, as in mixed-methods research, the researcher can validate findings from qualitative data, explore relationships, statistically represent results, and simultaneously gain a more comprehensive understanding of the context and complexities arising from quantitative data outcomes. In such cases, quantitative and qualitative research approaches tend to complement each other.

Qualitative and quantitative data collection techniques and data analysis

Interviews and surveys

Semi-structured interviews were conducted to collect primary qualitative data. Semi-structured interviews allowed the collection of richer and higher-quality data to understand the impact of AI on business postgraduate students' learning in higher education institutions in the UK, and more specifically, to understand which AI tools are more suited for each learning mode, the impact they have on learning, and the ethical implications brought on as a result of these tools. According to Magaldi and Berler (2020), although semi-structured interviews can be time-consuming to analyse and are subject to low objectivity and biases, they were suitable for this research because they allowed the interviewees more flexibility to respond, engage, and probe interesting areas and comments.

Furthermore, a structured survey was designed to generate quantitative results through the qualitative data collected. The survey included mainly closed-ended questions and matrix questions, and only one open-ended question to understand the impact of AI on business postgraduate students' learning in higher education institutions in the UK. The researcher ensured that the survey questions included all the possible responses to give the participants all the options. The survey allowed for more responses to be generated compared to the interviews in a shorter and cost-effective way.

In line with the nature and purpose of this research, to explore, examine, and evaluate the impact of AI, one semi-structured interview was carried out with (1) MBA students and (2) MBA academics/professionals. All interviews were conducted in English; therefore, there was no need for translation. The interviews took place on a one-to-one basis and online using Zoom. The participants were purposely sampled from the MBA students, as more mature and more experienced learners who had been part of the educational environment for a longer time than undergraduate students, and therefore with potentially more exposure to technology and AI in higher education institutions in the UK. Moreover, MBA academics/professionals were interviewed to explore different points of view in terms of the impact that AI has on business postgraduate students' learning in these institutions.

Furthermore, in line with the purpose of the research, one survey was designed and carried out with (1) MBA students from different higher education institutions in the UK and (2) MBA academics/professionals from different higher education institutions in the UK. The survey was designed using Jisc Online Surveys and was sent out to MBA students and academics/professionals across higher education institutions in the UK. The participants were purposely sampled as more experienced learners/academics, who had been engaged in learning environments for a longer time and, therefore, had been exposed to AI and AI tools more often. Some of the items of the survey were:

Due to the exploratory nature of this research, the non-probability sampling techniques have been implemented. Individuals are selected based on non-random criteria. The non-probability sampling technique used for this research is the purposive (judgemental) technique, which allows the selection of the participants based on some judgement and expertise to select a sample that is most useful for the research and to be able to better match the sample with the aims and objectives of the research. It increases the trustworthiness of the data and findings and improves the rigour of the research. Led by this understanding, the consent of the informants was gained, and they were interviewed. Consent was also gained from the participants who completed the survey.

Data analysis

Ando et al. (2014) define thematic analysis as the identification of a saturated set of themes and a meaningful "codebook" or other compilation of findings that documents the structure of codes and themes, with the validity of the findings paramount. Thematic analysis is the most common form of analysis in qualitative research; it can be applied when using a range of theories and epistemological approaches, and it is a simple and useful way to reflect and clarify reality. It is clear, uncomplicated, flexible, and it allows less experienced researchers to utilise it due to the high level of tangibility of the analysis phase. The identified themes can be presented in maps, representing a certain hierarchy or process. Thematic analysis is an easy data analysis technique to use; it allows the general public to understand the results generated from this method easily and helps the researcher to understand and explore experiences, behaviours, and thoughts across data sets; however, there are pitfalls related to this method too (Kiger & Varpio, 2020). Pitfalls include difficulties that describe the assumptions that underlie the analysis, it requires interpretive work, not just descriptions, and it may lack internal consistency when themes overlap. The researcher used thematic analysis to analyse the transcribed interviews to identify the themes, interpret them, and generate findings.

Puteh and Ong (2017) state that quantitative data analysis in the social science discipline offers another method of studying the environment around us, and it enables social scientists to measure, analyse, and understand the social reality. Scientific measurements are also employed in the social science discipline to ensure more accurate and reliable data analysis. There are two common theories used in statistical disciplines: the comparison statistical analysis theory and the correlation statistical analysis theory. For the purpose of this research, the comparison statistical analysis theory has been applied, and more specifically, the univariate analysis. According to Pallant (2015), univariate analysis refers to the analysis of one variable at a time. It involves a comparison analysis of one variable against several different groups. This analysis method was applicable for this research, as variables within the survey have been compared against three attributes: gender, age, and background. Statistical analysis can be performed using different statistical software; however, for this research, SPSS has been used as one of the most user-friendly platforms. SPSS is the preferred software used worldwide to analyse data through comparison and correlation statistical tests.

Descriptive statistics serve the purpose of summarising a set of observations to convey a maximum amount of information in the simplest manner possible (Lund Research Ltd, 2018). There are three primary categories of descriptive statistics: frequency measures (count and percentage), central tendency measures (average, median, and mode), and variability or dispersion measures (variance, standard deviation, standard error, quartiles, interquartile range, percentiles, range, and coefficient of variation). These measures offer straightforward summaries about the sample and its characteristics. Frequency measures are typically employed for categorical data, whereas the others are applied to quantitative data. For this analysis, frequency statistics have been employed using counts and frequencies, considering that most of the quantitative data collected are categorical data. Frequency statistics involve the straightforward tallying of occurrences for each variable, like counting the number of males and females in a given sample or population, etc.

Furthermore, SPSS allowed the researcher to consider a more in-depth quantitative analysis using correlation statistical tests. Correlation tests are undeniably one of the most widely utilised statistical procedures, forming the foundation for numerous applications. The primary aim is to offer simplicity and ease of use while accommodating the computation of various correlation types. These include Pearson's correlation, Spearman's rank correlation, Kendall's rank correlation, distance correlation, percentage bend correlation, and more (Makowski et al., 2020). For the research, correlation was completed to understand the relationship between several questions/answers by the participants. Spearman's rank correlation has been used. Spearman's rank correlation is a non-parametric measure of correlation that equates to the Pearson correlation computed between the ranked scores of two variables. While Pearson's correlation examines linear relationships, Spearman's correlation evaluates monotonic relationships, whether they are linear or not.

Additionally, Fisher-Freeman-Halton Exact Test has been employed to investigate if there was a significant association between two categorical variables. This test has been applied instead of correlation analysis to investigate the association between questions with different numbers of categories, in this case, questions 14 through 14k, that have two categories each, with question 16, which has five categories. In this case, Fisher's exact test was deemed more appropriate than the chi-square test due to many cells with a count of less than 5. Pearson's asymptotic Chi-square test is acceptable when no more than 20% of the cells have expected count less than 5. In the particular case, there were more than 20% of the cells with counts of less than 5; therefore, Fisher's test was more exact and less of an approximation.

Finally, another test employed as part of correlation statistics is the Wilcoxon signed rank test. It is a non-parametric statistical procedure that operates without the assumption of a normal distribution (Haynes, 2013). It serves the purpose of comparing two correlated samples, matched samples, or conducting a paired difference assessment of recurring measurements within a single sample to ascertain if there are disparities in their population mean ranks. Essentially, the Wilcoxon signed rank test represents the most basic manifestation of a repeated measures design. In research, it is quite common to employ multiple comparisons with repeated measures.

Ethical considerations

Ethical concerns arise during research in the designing and planning stage, as well as while accessing organisations and data collection and analysis processes. Therefore, research ethics should be taken into consideration throughout the process. The following ethical considerations were considered. The research project was subject to approval by the following: (1) Coventry University Ethics Committee, (2) Research Ethical Guidelines for Postgraduate Students, and (3) Coventry University's Business School's Research Ethics Committee Guidelines.

According to the Institutional Review Board (2022), informed consent aims at fully disclosing the nature of the research, the involvement of the participants, and the voluntary choice of the participants to be part of the research. Primarily, the researcher obtained consent from all the interviewees before attending the interview by allowing them to fill in a consent form. The consent form informed the participants about the purpose of the interview/ survey, the contact details of the researcher, and a statement of confidentiality, anonymity, and voluntary participation. The consent form was accompanied by a Participant Information Sheet, which further detailed the purpose of the research, the approximate time for its completion, a confidentiality and anonymity statement, data storage and ethical approval information, and the contact details of the researcher. The forms allowed promotion of transparency by the researcher and facilitated the interview process and survey completion.

Finally, participants of this research were made aware that their participation was entirely voluntary. The participants were informed of their opportunity to refuse participation in the research before or at any point during the research without any negative repercussions, as long as the data analysis process was not completed. Confidentiality, anonymity, and privacy were all emphasised in this research.

Conclusion

This chapter has presented a rigorous methodological framework for exploring how AI influences postgraduate business students' learning experiences in UK higher education. Grounded in critical realism, the mixed-methods design enabled the integration of empirical and experiential insights, balancing qualitative richness with quantitative precision. The adoption of triangulation, transparency, and ethical integrity ensured the study's validity, dependability, and credibility. By combining inductive reasoning with a robust data collection strategy, the research establishes a strong foundation for the subsequent analysis and discussion of findings, offering a comprehensive and trustworthy basis for understanding the evolving relationship between AI and higher education learning practices.

Reference list

Abu-Alhaiya, A. (2019). From epistemology to structural equation modelling: An essential guide in understanding the principles of research philosophy in selecting the appropriate methodology. *Australian Journal of Basic and Applied Sciences*, *13*(9), 122–128.

Al-Ababneh, M. (2020). Linking ontology, epistemology and research methodology. *Science & Philosophy*, *8*(1), 75–91. SSRN. https://ssrn.com/abstract=3708935

Alharahsheh, H. H., & Pius, A. (2020). A review of key paradigms: Positivism VS interpretivism. *Global Academic Journal of Humanities and Social Sciences*, 2(3), 39–43.

Ando, H., Cousins, R., & Young, C. (2014). Achieving saturation in thematic analysis: Development and refinement of a codebook. *Comprehensive Psychology*, *3*, Article 4.

Armstrong, R. (2019). Elaborating a critical realist approach to soft systems methodology. *Systemic Practice and Action Research*, *32*, 463–480. https://doi.org/10.1007/s11213-018-9466-7

Baldwin, L. (2018). *Research concepts for the practitioner of educational leadership* (1st ed., pp. 31–36). Brill.

Bell, E., Bryman, A., & Harley, B. (2022). *Business research methods* (6th ed.). Oxford University Press.

Bellido-Garcia, R., Cruzata-Martinez, A., Ponce, M., Rejas, B., & Gerardo, L. (2022). Implicit theories on learning assessments and the use of triangulation as a means of qualitative validity and reliability. *EBSCO*, *27*(5), 1276–1300.

Burns, A. (2010). Action research. In B. Paltridge & A. Phakiti (Eds.), *Continuum companion to research methods in applied linguistics* (pp. 80–97). Continuum.

Chalhoub-Deville, M., Chapelle, C. A., & Duff, P. A. (2006). *Inference and generalizability in applied linguistics: Multiple perspectives* (Vol. 12). John Benjamins Publishing.

Corley, K., Bansal, P. (Tima), & Yu, H. (2021). An editorial perspective on judging the quality of inductive research when the methodological straightjacket is loosened. *Strategic Organization*, *19*(1), 161–175. https://doi.org/10.1177/1476127020968180

Haynes, W. (2013). *Wilcoxon rank sum test* (pp. 2354–2355). Springer New York.

Hays, D., & McKibben, W. (2021). Promoting rigorous research: Generalizability and qualitative research. *Journal of Counselling & Development*, *99*(2), 178–188.

Hoddy, E. T. (2019). Critical realism in empirical research: Employing techniques from grounded theory methodology. *International Journal of Social Research Methodology*, *22*(1), 111–124.

Institutional Review Board. (2022). *Required components of informed consent.* Retrieved October 31, 2025, from https://www.irb.cornell.edu/forms/consent.htm

Kiger, M. E., & Varpio, L. (2020). Thematic analysis of qualitative data: AMEE Guide No. 131. *Medical Teacher*, *42*(8), 846–854.

Kyngäs, H., Kääriäinen, M., & Elo, S. (2020). The trustworthiness of content analysis. In H. Kyngäs, K. Mikkonen, & M. Kääriäinen (Eds.), *The application of content analysis in nursing science research*. Springer. https://doi.org/10.1007/978-3-030-30199-6_5

Lund Research Ltd. (2018). *Descriptive and inferential statistics.* Retrieved October 31, 2025, from http://www.statistics.laerd.com

Magaldi, D., & Berler, M. (2020). Semi-structured interviews. In V. Zeigler-Hill & T. K. Shackelford (Eds.), *Encyclopedia of personality and individual differences.* Springer. https://doi.org/10.1007/978-3-319-24612-3_857

Makowski, D., Ben-Shachar, M. S., Patil, I., & Lüdecke, D. (2020). Methods and algorithms for correlation analysis in R. *Journal of Open Source Software*, *5*(51), 2306.

Merriam, S. B. (2009). *Qualitative research: A guide to design and implementation* (2nd ed.). Jossey-Bass.

Mukumbang, F. C. (2021). Retroductive theorizing: A contribution of critical realism to mixed methods research. *Journal of Mixed Methods Research.* https://doi.org/10.1177/15586898211049847

Noble, H., & Heale, R. (2019). Triangulation in research, with examples. *Evidence-based Nursing*, *22*(3), 67–68.

Nunan, D., & Bailey, K. M. (2009). *Exploring second language classroom research: A comprehensive guide.* Heinle, Cengage Learning.

Ogeyik, M., & Uzun, K. (2022). *Language, society, history, economy and politics in social sciences* (1st ed., pp. 155–156). Özgür Yayınları.

Pallant, J. (2015). *SPSS survival manual.* Open University Press.

Puteh, F., & Ong, M. (2017). Quantitative data analysis: Choosing between SPSS, PLS and AMOS in social science research. *International Interdisciplinary Journal of Scientific Research*, *3*(1).

Renz, S. M., Carrington, J. M., & Badger, T. A. (2018). Two strategies for qualitative content analysis: An intramethod approach to triangulation. *Qualitative Health Research*, *5*, 824–831.

Sharifah, I. S. S. (2020). Extending the concept of pro-environmental action and behaviour: A binary perspective. *Environmental Education Research*, *26*(12), 1764–1786. https://doi.org/10.1080/13504622.2020.1850645

Shenton, & Andrew, K. (2004). Strategies for ensuring trustworthiness in qualitative research projects. *Education for Information*, *22*(2), 63–75. https://doi.org/10.3233/EFI-2004-22201

Silverman, D. (2006). *Interpreting qualitative data: Methods for analyzing talk, text, and interaction* (3rd ed.). Sage.

Stahl, N. A., & King, J. R. (2020). Expanding approaches for research: Understanding and using trustworthiness in qualitative research. *Journal of Developmental Education*, *44*(1), 26–28.

Stumpfegger, E. (2017). *Trustworthiness of research. MBS insights.* [online] Retrieved October 31, 2025, from https://www.munich-business-school.de/insights/en/2017/trustworthiness-of-research/

Stutchbury, K. (2022). Critical realism: An explanatory framework for small-scale qualitative studies or an 'unhelpful edifice'? *International Journal of Research & Method in Education*, *45*(2), 113–128. https://doi.org/10.1080/1743727X.2021.1966623

Trochim, W. M. (2006). *Social research methods*. Retrieved from Research Methods Knowledge Base. https://www.socialresearchmethods.net/

Vu, T. T. N. (2021). Understanding validity and reliability from qualitative and quantitative research traditions. *VNU Journal of Foreign Studies*, *37*(3).

Wolcott, H. F. (2005). *The art of fieldwork*. Alta Mira Press.

6 AI's impact on business postgraduate learning in UK higher education

Introduction

This chapter examines the role and influence of AI on business postgraduate learning within UK higher education. Drawing on both interview and survey data from MBA students and academic staff, the discussion explores how AI tools are currently being applied across various learning modes and how these tools impact students' learning experiences. The chapter also considers students' and academics' perceptions of the benefits and challenges associated with AI, alongside the ethical implications that arise from its use. By analysing both the pedagogical and ethical dimensions, the chapter provides an informed understanding of how AI can support and shape postgraduate business education in a rapidly evolving digital landscape.

Participants' demographic characteristics

Interview participants' demographic characteristics

The sample for this research consisted of 13 participants (students: n=8 and academics/professionals n=5). All the participating students were MBA students studying in higher education institutions in the UK, and all the participating academics/professionals were working within the MBA departments in the Business Schools of six higher education institutions in the UK. The dominant age groups for students are 26–29 and 36–39, and the dominant groups for academics/professionals are 40–45 and above 50. Out of the total, 37.5% of the students belong to the age group of 26–29, and the same percentage belongs to the age group of 36–39. The rest is also equally distributed into two age brackets, 18–25 and 30–35, 12.5% each. No students belonged to the age groups of 40–45, 46–49, or above 50. On the other hand, the opposite applies to academics/professionals who belong to two age groups only, 40–45 and 50+, with a dominant category of 60% in the 40–45 bracket. In terms of gender distributions, most student participants were females (87.5%), whereas most academics/professionals, 60% were males. Additionally, participants were distributed on the basis of their region

DOI: 10.4324/9781003664161-6

of the world they came from. The results show that most of the students were from the Asian continent, 75% and only 25% were from Africa. None of the students were from Europe, America, or Australia. On the other hand, most academics/professionals, 60%, came from Europe, and the remaining were equally distributed amongst two other continents, Asia and South America, 20% each. No academics/professionals came from Africa or Australia. Finally, participants were distributed based on the region they were currently studying (for students) or working (for academics/professionals). Students were equally distributed amongst two regions only, the West Midlands and Greater London, 50% each. On the other hand, academics/professionals who participated in the interviews/survey were part of higher education institutions in the West Midlands only.

Survey participants' demographic characteristics

In terms of the demographics of the survey participants, the sample for this research consisted of 47 participants (students: n=38 and academics/professionals n=9). All the participating students were MBA students studying in higher education institutions in the UK, and all the participating academics/professionals were working within the MBA departments in the Business Schools of several higher education institutions in the UK. In terms of gender and background, the majority of participants consists of students and females; however, 19.1% of the participants are males, and 19.1% are academics/professionals; therefore, these two groups are represented in the responses and the findings. In terms of age and region respondents come from, there is a higher response rate from younger individuals, compared to older age groups, and most participants are originally from Europe and Asia. Finally, the participants study or work mainly in England, and a lower number of participants are from the other regions of the UK, such as Wales, Scotland, and Northern Ireland. Previous research completed on reasons why certain groups participate more or less in online surveys has been highlighted hereafter for each category, similar to the interview responses.

The results suggest that the age distribution of the survey participants, the majority, 34%, belong to the age group of 30–35 years; followed by 29.8% that belong to the age group 26–29 years. It has been noted that no participants belong to the age group 46–49, and only 2.1% of the participants are 50+ years old. The rest belong to the three other age groups, 18–25, 36–39, and 40–45. Williams (2008) supports the above by stating that younger people are more likely to participate in online questionnaires than older people. Furthermore, Mulder and de Bruijne (2019) argue that younger people prefer web-based data collection methods, whereas older people prefer non-web modes, thus leading to a lower response rate when questionnaires are completed online.

In terms of gender, it is clearly distinguished that most of the respondents are females, dominating with 80.9% of the total. Only 19.1% of the respondents are males. It shows that female participants have been more willing to complete the survey compared to males. Research conducted by Williams (2008) on understanding whether gender influences online survey participation discovered that women are more likely to participate in these surveys than men due to differences in female and male values. While males highly value separative characteristics, females, on the other hand, value characteristics such as empathy and emotional closeness. Additionally, more recent research suggests that men are less likely to respond in surveys than women. Women are more likely to respond promptly after the invitation to participate in online surveys, compared to men (Becker, 2022). Slauson-Blevins and Johnson (2016) highlight that even though the overall response rates for online surveys are declining, the gender effect on the rate of survey participation remains clear.

Of the participants who completed the survey, 80.9% are MBA students, and 19.1% of the participants are academics/professionals working within the MBA departments of Business Schools in higher education institutions in the UK. Academics/professionals, as working and busy individuals, were harder to connect with, and therefore it was less possible to fill in the survey by a larger number.

Findings suggest that most of the survey respondents are studying MBA or working within the MBA team in England, particularly in the Greater London area (36.2%), followed by the West Midlands with 34%. The rest of the respondents are distributed amongst West of England and Scotland (8.5% each), Wales (6.4%), East of England (4.3%), and East Midlands (2.1%). According to Dhariyal (2021), amongst the top 30 MBA colleges in the UK in 2021, 26 of them are based in England, 3 in Scotland, and 1 in Wales. Considering this and the high number of Business Schools and MBA programmes in England, the highest numbers of MBA students in the UK are located in England. Therefore, the highest numbers of participants for this survey are located in the regions of England, mainly Greater London and the West Midlands. Although the majority study or work in England, the sample is still representative of the other regions in the UK.

Finally, most participants are from Asia (38.3%) and Europe (34%), followed by Africa with 21.3%. The remaining respondents are from North and South America, accounting for 4.3% and 2.1%, respectively. The difference between the regions is high; however, this is expected given that most of the UK students come from Europe and England, Asia, and Africa. Research conducted by the Higher Education Statistics Agency (HESA, 2022) revealed that the number of overseas students in the UK increased by 34% from 2016 to 2021. China and India remain the most dominant countries from which international students originate, followed by a notable growth from countries such as Pakistan and Nigeria.

AI technologies and their suitability for different learning modes

Interview analysis and results

Current applicability of AI systems in higher education institutions in the UK has been identified as the first theme from the interviews, with the intention of understanding what AI systems/tools higher education institutions in the UK have currently applied to support students' learning. This served as the basis for further understanding the most suitable tools and systems that can be applied to the four identified learning modes: face-to-face learning, online learning, demonstration and feedback, and independent learning. Participants generally demonstrated a moderate understanding of the types of AI systems and tools implemented within their higher education institutions. However, several participants expressed uncertainty about the specific technologies in use or whether certain systems could accurately be classified as AI. Notably, three of the 13 student participants indicated limited awareness or confidence regarding the AI tools available to them. The following examples illustrate this variation in understanding.

> *"I'm sure there were a lot of them in the background, of course we weren't told that this is functioning for you right now but one I can think of right off the bat is Teledyne, that's an AI tool to detect plagiarism".*
>
> *"No, I don't think so. AI, do you want to talk about the website or the app, which helps us for interaction of the sessions, I don't think that comes into AI. Does it come to AI?"*
>
> *"No, I don't use any".*

From the responses of the interviewees, 19 types of AI tools/systems were identified and it can be recognised that 11 of the tools are specific systems that are used within higher education institutions to assist students' learning. These include Future Learn, Insights Discovery, Locate, Mintel, My.wbs, Otter, ProQuest, RapidMiner, Scopus, Teledyne, and VMock. The remaining AI tools identified from the responses focus on general systems that are used to support students' learning within higher education institutions in the UK. These include feedback tools, engineering department tools, algorithm-based tools, business intelligence tools, 24/7 chatbots, data analytics tools, simulation-based tools, VR, and augmented reality tools.

To further explore the most suitable AI technologies for each identified learning mode, thematic analysis of the findings from the interviews has been completed in this section. Analysis of existing literature identified four main learning modes, which students use to learn in higher education institutions in the UK: face-to-face learning, online learning, demonstration and feedback, and independent learning. The analysis recognised that most of the tools (n=23) would be applicable to be used for face-to-face learning, followed by n=15 for online learning, n=6 for independent learning, and n=2 for demonstration and feedback.

According to Pangaribuan et al. (2022), demonstration method motivates students to participate in learning, and instead of being passive, they contribute and are active throughout the lessons. During the interviews, participants showed greater interest in identifying AI tools and systems used in face-to-face and online learning modes, while considerably less emphasis was placed on those supporting demonstration, feedback, and independent learning. As a result, only two AI tools were recognised as relevant to demonstration and learning contexts. Specifically, feedback-oriented and guidance-based AI tools were identified as the primary applications that could be integrated into these modes to enhance students' learning experiences.

Hattie (2019) argues that face-to-face learning utilises support to guide students during their learning process by ensuring that they have been clearly explained the purpose of learning the new skills and supported with feedback till independence is accomplished. A considerable number of references were identified from the responses of the interviewees (n=23) from ten different files. AI tools have been considered as powerful systems that support face-to-face learning more than all the other learning modes, and they focus mainly on the provision of feedback, inclusion, well-being, 24/7 support, personalised learning, and student satisfaction.

Singh and Thurman (2019) highlight that online learning allows students to learn and interact with instructors and other students from any place and independently. The analysis recognised 13 types of AI tools/systems that can support students in the online learning mode. The findings from the above analysis demonstrate that the participants consider the online learning mode as the second most important mode after the face-to-face learning, in which AI tools/systems can be implemented to support students' learning. The systems suggested to be implemented for this learning mode vary; however, the main focus is on personalised chatbots, well-being, feedback, diversification, and mental health.

According to Naibaho (2019), an independent learning mode is a learning strategy that aims to build individual initiative, independence, and self-improvement, strongly built by the students' learning motivation. When students study independently, they initially use low-level organising and reinforcing skills, and later on, they develop higher-level applying and extending skills. The analysis identified six AI tools/systems that were considered important to be applied and used to support students' learning while studying independently. Having taken into consideration the fact that this particular learning mode allows students to learn independently, the focus of systems identified by the participants is on interaction, guidance, feedback, and the opportunity to have their questions answered. According to Han (2017), students receive very little instruction and organisation from teachers while studying independently; hence, the need for appropriate resources for learning increases. Independent learners require more support, guidance, and advice; thus, AI tools and systems identified are useful resources to support independent learners through personalised guidance, interaction, and assistance.

From the interviews, it became clear that most participants saw AI as a useful addition to the learning process, no matter the mode of study. Whether students were learning face to face, online, independently, or through demonstration and feedback, there was a general sense that AI tools could play a supportive role. Even so, the strongest attention was given to face-to-face and online learning, which participants described as the most immediate contexts for AI integration. One tool, however, stood out across every learning mode: the feedback system. Many participants pointed out that feedback is essential to their learning and that automated AI systems could help provide it more quickly and consistently. They felt that having instant access, personalised feedback helps them understand their progress and stay engaged, even when studying on their own. Another recurring point was the use of chatbots to answer common student queries. These were seen as particularly helpful for those studying face to face, online, or independently, as they reduce delays in communication and make information more accessible. More similarities have been identified between the face-to-face mode and online learning, with well-being, mental health, and personalised support being the key areas that AI can support. Participants raised mental health and well-being as an important aspect of learning that affects students significantly; therefore, the need for automated AI systems that consider students' well-being and mental health has been elevated for both online and face-to-face learning modes. According to Kuhail et al. (2024), universities are sometimes stretched to capacity, and students have to wait longer than they should to be provided with counselling services; therefore, AI chatbots are able to help students manage their mental well-being quickly. Another important area of support provided by AI was identified in three of the learning modes, face-to-face, online, and independent, and it is personalised support. Interviewees identified personalised chatbots as relevant to support students' learning. The chatbots should be personalised based on students' culture, empathy levels, their capacity, as well as their wants. Findings suggest that these chatbots are most relevant for students who study online and in classrooms. Furthermore, it was considered that personalised support is important for those who study independently by identifying personalised guidance, interaction, and personalised scheduling assistance as the most important features of the AI systems that should be available for independent learners. To conclude, in addition to similarities, differences in the AI tools and systems have been identified for the four learning modes. Unique automated systems have been considered by the participants based on the characteristics of each learning mode. Analysis demonstrates that for independent learners, it is important that tools should be able to assist with scheduling and should interact with students due to the nature of this learning mode, where studying alone and independently is always required. Furthermore, students who study online should have the option to access pre-class materials through automated systems before attending the lecture online to be able to prepare relevant questions. In addition, students who study face to face would benefit from AI tools that provide 24/7 library functions and academic and registry support to avoid queues and reduce waiting times. Moreover, they would benefit from tools that produce predictive scenarios in classrooms, allow real-time interaction, and ease conversations with teachers.

Survey analysis and results

To explore the views of the participants related to which AI technologies would be most appropriate and applicable for each learning mode, the following five identified modes were listed: explicit learning (traditional, face-to-face), online learning, demonstration, feedback and reflection, and independent learning mode. On the other hand, seven popular AI tools/systems were considered: (1) Teacherbots: virtual teachers; (2) Chatbots: answer general questions; (3) Woebot: help students to understand emotions; (4) Smart Sparrow: online platform (content- and experiments-based); (5) STEVE: Intelligent Tutoring System (physical and procedural tasks available); (6) D2L (Desire 2 Learn): Online platform (available content, material, tests; provides feedback; analyses learning; predicts courses); (7) Yixue Squirrel AI: chatbot that provides individualised feedback based on behaviour. The findings comprise analysis of each learning mode, to understand which of the above tools is the most applicable and which is less applicable for the particular mode.

Face-to-face—The analysis suggests that the most selected AI tool for this mode is STEVE, the intelligent tutoring system that provides physical and procedural tasks. Of the participants, 46.8% believe that STEVE would be the most appropriate for the traditional face-to-face learning mode, followed by the virtual teachers with 27.7%. On the other hand, D2L is the least selected tool for face-to-face learning; only 14.9% of the participants relate this tool to this particular mode. The remaining five tools/systems have been almost equally selected by the respondents, with percentages varying from 14.9% to 21.3%. According to Goenka et al. (2021), the main purpose of STEVE is interaction with students; thus, it can easily support face-to-face learning where real-time interaction between students and between students and teachers is key. On the other hand, D2L has been the least selected given that it focuses on providing online content and online feedback, which in this learning mode can be done face to face.

Online learning—The analysis demonstrates that the virtual teachers and D2L are the most selected AI tools for the online learning mode, with 59.6% and 55.3% responses, respectively. Smart Sparrow and Yixue Squirrel follow on with 34% responses each, and chatbots with 31.9%. The least selected tool is the Woebot with 21.3%. The findings suggest that teacherbots should be considered as a key AI tool to support the online learning mode, given that teacherbots can play the role of a teacher throughout the duration of a course. Furthermore, D2L and Smart Sparrow have been selected, providing that they are online platforms that allow students to access content, tests, experiments, etc. (Wan, 2020). Online students do not have the opportunity to study face to face; therefore, having access to platforms where all is available would be very convenient.

Demonstration—The analysis shows that Smart Sparrow is the most selected to suit the demonstration learning mode, with more than 48% responses, given that it offers a great number of simulation experiments, such as designing virtual buildings and complex virtual surgeries to allow students to "learn by doing" (Smart Sparrow, 2022; Wan, 2020). Smart Sparrow is followed by STEVE with a 42.6% rate of selection. Providing that demonstration is defined as the process of showing something, for example, ideas, concepts, processes, arguments, and visualisations, through reason and/or proof and clarifying with examples, experiments, and steps (NSW Education, 2020), STEVE has been seen as a suitable choice due to its ability to show and explain students how to complete physical and procedural tasks and assist and instruct them as necessary (Goenka et al., 2021). Woebot and chatbots are the least selected options with 8.5% and 10.6%, respectively, considering that they focus on emotions and answering questions, and the main focus of demonstration mode is to show rather than tell.

Feedback and reflection—The findings suggest that Yixue Squirrel Artificial Intelligence chatbot is the most appropriate suggested tool to support this learning mode due to its ability to collect and analyse data related to students' behaviour and provide timely individualised feedback (Squirrel AI, 2022). Following on, D2L and Woebot are equally selected with a 38% rate of response by the participants. According to NSW Education (2020), through feedback and reflection learning mode, students are able to obtain feedback from their classroom friends, their teachers, and other physical and non-physical elements; therefore, D2L and Woebot are seen as suitable given that Woebot helps students to reflect on their emotions (Dhawan, 2021) and D2L provides feedback on learning and allows students to understand their current progress and the areas for improvement. Smart Sparrow is the least selected tool (8.5%), considering it is highly focused on experiments and content provision.

Independent learning—The analysis suggests that 51.1% of the responses consider D2L as the most appropriate platform for independent learning because it provides a very comprehensive range of services for students, including assignment submission, practice test questions, reading course materials, communicating with each other, analysing learning and providing feedback, and predicting courses that are suitable for students' progress (D2L, 2022). Providing that independent learning is an autonomous mode of learning and requires self-organisation and self-regulation, a platform like D2L that provides an all-in-one service would be very suitable. The least selected AI tool is Woebot; nevertheless, still 23.4% of the responses consider it appropriate for independent learning, given that it considers student emotions. The remaining five tools have all been highly considered by the participants, with a range of responses between 36.2% and 42.6%. Given that independent learning is characterised by independent studies, self-organisation, self-regulation, independently finding solutions for different problems, and making difficult decisions related to learning (NSW Education, 2020), participants believe that all AI tools suggested are suitable for students because of the high level of support that independent learners require.

Summary

The five identified learning modes included in the survey question consist of explicit (face-to-face), online, demonstration, feedback and reflection, and independent learning mode. The same five learning modes were used in the interview questions; nevertheless, due to the low number of responses, the demonstration and feedback learning modes have been merged into one category, given that only two responses were provided. The interview allowed the participants to explore different answers, whereas the survey questions were quite structured; therefore, the participants had to choose among the options available. Consequently, the AI systems and tools suggested for each learning mode are not the same in the survey and the interviews; however, they are similar as they provide similar services for students and their learning. The systems identified from the interview responses are general technologies mainly, with a few specific names, whereas the survey included specific AI tools and systems. Similarly, more tools and systems have been identified through the responses of the interviews, due to the semi-structured nature of the interview and its flexibility in terms of time and length of answers. On the other hand, fewer options were made available in the survey question, given that a survey should take less time to complete than an interview. Finally, the main focus of the interviewees was the face-to-face learning and online mode of learning; therefore, fewer responses have been identified for the independent learning mode, demonstration, and feedback. Conversely, in the survey, the identified AI tools and systems for each learning mode are equal in number due to the fixed number of options available. No triangulation of these findings with the existing literature has been completed for the first part of this objective due to the lack of data available concerning which AI tools are most suitable for each identified learning mode. Although several researchers argue that AI has been widely applied in higher education and used to support students' learning in any learning mode (Ouyang & Jiao, 2021), no specific research has been completed related to the most suitable AI technologies for each learning mode separately; therefore, all the findings from the interviews and the survey are new and add to the existing literature.

Demonstration and feedback learning modes have been less considered by the participants, and only two types of AI systems are identified from the interview responses: feedback tools and guiding tools. These findings align with the survey results for the following reason: participants who completed the survey identified Smart Sparrow, STEVE, and teacherbots as the key tools to use for the demonstration learning mode. All three guide students through available experiments, physical demonstrations, and guiding replies. Similarly, Yixue Squirrel and D2L were mainly identified for the feedback learning mode due to their ability to provide individualised feedback to students. In summary, all the specific tools identified through the survey responses confirm the two key AI technologies in the interviews, feedback, and guiding tools.

The interviewees considered the independent learning mode more than demonstration and feedback; therefore, more responses were identified through the interviews, mainly concerning feedback tools, assignment submission tools, chatbots for general queries, guiding, interaction, and scheduling assistants. Same as with the two previous learning modes, the findings from the interview align with the survey findings. The key tools identified through the survey include D2L, STEVE, teacherbots, and chatbots. D2L is a platform that provides both feedback and the possibility to submit assignments and take practice tests. Chatbots for general queries have been identified in both sets of data collected. STEVE and teacherbots can provide guidance, interact with the students, and assist them with particular tasks, such as scheduling, if needed.

Online learning mode is considered an important learning mode where students would benefit from a range of AI tools and systems identified in the survey and interview. The main focus of the tools identified through the interviews is around systems that provide diversified solutions, pre-class content and material, feedback, as well as chatbots for general queries, personalised bots, mental health and well-being bots, and tools that help put theory to practice. The findings from the interviews align with the findings from the survey, considering that the most selected AI tools and platforms are: D2L, STEVE, Chatbots, Yixue, etc. D2L is a platform that provides diversified solutions through a range of services such as content and material, practice tests, personalised feedback, and prediction of courses. STEVE can put theory into practice by providing physical demonstrations of tasks and experiments. Woebot helps students with emotions, thus contributing to their mental health and well-being positively.

Face-to-face is the mode of learning mainly considered by the interviewees as learning that would highly benefit from the application of a variety of AI tools and systems. The findings from the interviews suggest that the AI technologies that would best support students who study face to face include the following: 24/7 library functions, academic and registry support, chatbots, personalised content and material, feedback tools, inclusive learning tools, open-source platforms, etc. These findings align with the findings from the survey, where participants have considered tools such as STEVE, teacherbots, Yixue Squirrel, and chatbots as the main technologies that would support students' learning. STEVE, as an intelligent tutoring system, focuses on creating a collaborative environment for students by not only demonstrating the tasks but also monitoring the students' performance after the task's completion. Teacherbots can play the role of a teacher throughout the duration of a course and deal generally with automated tasks such as content delivery, basic feedback, and supervision, as well as providing a personalised teaching experience for students. Yixue Squirrel focuses on feedback too, and chatbots assist students with responding to general queries, including library functions. Given that the interview allows for open responses and gives students more time and flexibility in their answers, the findings from the interview concerning the face-to-face mode of learning have identified a few more AI technologies that could support students' learning, which are not included in the survey. These include IQ improvement AI tools, tools that ease conversations between teachers and students, pragmatic situations analytical tools, and asynchronous tasks tools.

To conclude, the findings from the interviews and the survey that accomplish the first objective of this research align and complement each other. It has been noted that personalised learning is one of the main features that AI brings to students in higher education institutions, as evident in the existing literature, as well as in the findings from interviews and surveys. Ali et al. (2025) define personalised learning as a variety of educational programs in which the pace of learning and the instructional approach are customised and eventually optimised for the needs of each learner; in particular, the content is tailored to the learning preferences and specific interests of each student. Due to the recent advancements in AI technology, the interest of higher education in it is increasing, given the rise in demand for flexible, customised, and self-directed learning. Furthermore, traditional learning focuses more on the "one size fits all" approach, where the differences amongst students cannot be considered; therefore, AI attempts to resolve this problem by providing an on-demand, customised learning experience (Al-Badi et al., 2022).

The impact of AI systems/tools on business postgraduate students' learning

Interview analysis and results

The analysis on the impact of AI tools and systems on business postgraduate students' learning generated three main sub-themes from the interviews: positive impact, negative impact, and equally positive and negative.

Positive impact—Thematic analysis of the interviews demonstrated that participants consider AI tools and systems to have a more positive than negative impact on business postgraduate students' learning for several reasons, which have been categorised into 15 groups as follows: access, personalised services, flexibility, efficiency, interactivity, speed, inclusion, transparency, fairness, convenience, accuracy, satisfaction, self-awareness, bias, and cost.

Inclusion—Analysis demonstrates that the ability of AI systems and tools to endorse and stimulate inclusion is the main reason for generating a positive impact on students' learning. The responses of interviewees identified eight references that elaborate on how inclusion has a positive impact on learning. Inclusion is not only about including learners with special needs but also about including all learners. In its Global Education Monitoring Report, UNESCO (2020) highlights that inclusion in education is about ensuring that every learner feels valued and respected and can enjoy a clear sense of belonging. The findings from the interviews suggest that participants consider AI systems as important tools that could include not only students with disabilities but also students' constraints due to illnesses, countries' rules and regulations, and backgrounds; thus, having a positive impact on their learning.

Speed, efficiency, and accuracy—Furthermore, analysis demonstrates that AI tools and systems impact students' learning due to speed, efficiency, and accuracy. Participants identified these three reasons as vital in positively impacting students' learning. The analysis demonstrates that AI tools and systems improve access to learning; students have better and quicker access to academic and registry support, as well as improved access to resources, including people all around the world. Furthermore, AI tools provide students with quicker responses to queries, quicker marks due to automated marking, along with reduced need to stand in long queues to receive information. Likewise, the tools offer higher efficiency by avoiding repetition of information and wasting time by going from one human to the next. One of the benefits of AI is the speed of receiving responses, supported by the example of IBM's Watson, which answered more than 55,000 questions from students within the first 12 months of implementation. Abogunrin et al. (2025) support the above arguments by stating that AI is quick and efficient, as it allows a multitude of tasks to be completed quickly and efficiently.

Personalised services, interactivity, flexibility, convenience, and self-awareness—Additionally, thematic analysis identified further positive impact of AI tools on business postgraduate students' learning, including personalised services, interactivity, flexibility, convenience, and self-awareness. Analysis demonstrates that AI provides better insights for students on how to adapt learning technologies to their personal needs and identify user habits and behavioural patterns through the use of AI tools. Yixue Squirrel AI system is able to collect and analyse data related to students' behaviour and provide timely individualised feedback. Furthermore, AI impacts students' learning positively as it allows higher interaction levels with each other, a higher level of engagement during the learning process, flexibility related to learning at their own pace, and revisiting the material whenever time and availability allow. Zhao and Liu (2019) argue that Smart Sparrow is a platform that offers a rich, interactive, and adaptive educational content for students, and it involves several fields of study, such as science, engineering, medicine, etc., thus allowing a higher level of personalisation and interactivity. Using AI tools within higher education institutions produces further positive impact by allowing a higher level of convenience for students learning through a better level of understanding of how to put knowledge into practice. Moreover, analysis shows that for students, it is more convenient to interact with AI tools than with humans. Intelligent tutoring systems, such as STEVE and ADELE, have the ability to understand what the student is doing and use their ability to act in response to students' actions to look more realistic, mindful of the user, and be able to motivate and influence students (Goenka et al., 2021). Self-awareness, as another benefit of AI on students' learning, allows students to improve their thinking and self-evaluate. The D2L platform provides beneficial feedback to students, which allows them to understand their current progress and the areas for improvement; thus, improving their thinking and self-evaluation.

Cost, bias, satisfaction, accuracy, fairness, and transparency—Finally, thematic analysis acknowledged further sub-themes which positively impact students' learning, including cost, bias, satisfaction, accuracy, fairness, and transparency. The findings suggest that each of them has been identified once by the participants. Findings also suggest that AI systems are considered as creating value for money due to all the positive impact and benefits they have on business postgraduate students' learning; however, this contradicts existing literature where Dhawan (2021) suggests that higher education institutions may result in increasing fees for students due to the high cost of AI implementation until a low-cost AI is achieved. Additionally, findings suggest that AI systems reduce human bias, which contradicts Professor Jan Willem de Graff (2019), who states that data is always a limited "reflection" (measurement) of a limited part of reality; in essence, it is always biased. High levels of accuracy and transparency have been identified as positively impacting students' learning within higher education institutions in the UK, accompanied by an improved students' satisfaction rate for the faculty. Finally, findings suggest that a system that implements AI is fairer than the current system, where AI is not fully integrated; however, Remian (2019) argues that AI systems cannot be accessed by many; therefore, they cannot be fair or equitable.

Negative impact—Thematic analysis identified the impact of AI to be negative as well as positive; nevertheless, the negative impact is significantly lower. It has been categorised into five sub-themes recognised through six references from the interviews. The analysis suggests that even though AI tools provide quicker grades through automated marking and quicker personalised feedback, they can still harm students' learning as a result of two key reasons. First, participants consider the marking of multiple-choice exams or assignments from automated AI systems as achievable and acceptable; however, marking essays and reports, which need to be understood and then provided with comments, could be challenging and not fully achieved; thus, leading to unsatisfied students. Second, the feedback provided by automated systems may not reflect reality due to the lack of ability of AI to understand meaning. Schiff (2021) argues that mathematics is a science that relies on standard equations and problem-solving procedures; therefore, it is easier for AI to model it. On the other hand, understanding meaning and context is far more challenging for the technology.

Additionally, findings suggest that constant usage of AI leads to dependence on the technology and potentially affects the memory negatively in the long term. As an example, the chatbot called Pounce, which is used at Georgia State University, reminds students by text regarding incomplete tasks. If students fully rely on this AI tool and the system develops technical issues, this may lead to students missing out on completing their tasks because of the reliance on AI and the inability to remember their own duties. Furthermore, findings propose that AI magnifies biases, which contradicts the previous findings, which suggest that AI reduces human biases as the process is fully automated. Finally, it has been noted that AI is not stable yet. It has developed to some extent; however, not enough to replace a teacher 100%, especially if we consider empathy as one of the main features that humans possess, but AI does not yet. Saputra et al. (2024) discuss the worrying possibility of teaching being replaced by AI, which could be profitable in the long run but just a superficial approach; whereas Tahir et al. (2024) argue that when AI reaches its ultimate vision, teachers will only be playing a passive role.

Equally positive and negative impact—The analysis identified two references from the responses of the interviewees that define the impact of AI on students' learning as equally positive and negative. The findings suggest that the impact can be equally positive and negative, as it depends on the communication style and approach. Examples that support the above finding include a student receiving quick personalised feedback on an assignment from an AI tool, which impacts their learning positively; on the other hand, the feedback received is not welcomed by the student due to the way it has been communicated to them, and an approach that does not take into consideration feelings and emotions.

Survey analysis and results

Personalised learning—Given that personalised learning has been identified as one of the main impacts of AI on business postgraduate students' learning, further analysis was completed. Participants' views on understanding in which of the learning modes students would benefit the most from personalised learning and the application of AI tools were considered. The overall findings suggest that all the identified learning modes would benefit from personalised learning and AI tools; however, feedback and reflection are the two most selected modes, with a response rate of 68.1% each. Online learning follows with 57.4%, explicit learning with 53.2%, and independent learning with 48.9%. The percentage values do not constitute a large difference between them. With a range from 48.9% to 68.1%, the results suggest that all learning modes would benefit from personalised learning, some slightly more than others.

Quality—Of the participants, 68.1% consider AI tools and systems to lead to higher-quality learning; on the other hand, 31.9% believe that these technologies lead to lower quality of learning. Overall, this finding suggests that the quality of learning, as one of the impacts of AI on learning, is affected by the technology, and most of the participants believe that the quality increases. This finding supports Farhan et al. (2024), who argue that AI applications in higher education can address previous quality issues.

Interactivity—Of the participants, 51.1% consider AI to lead to less interactive learning, whereas 48.9% consider a more interactive learning. Participants appear to be split into two half-groups when considering interactivity as an impact of AI on learning, with one group leaning more towards less interactive learning for students. Overall, this finding suggests that interactivity, as one of the impacts of AI on learning, is affected by the technology, and just less than half of the participants believe that interactivity increases. More than half consider AI to lead to less interactive learning. This finding supports Le Dinh et al. (2025), who argue that AI tools and systems lack emotions, feelings, and interactions due to being technology-centric and not human-centric. It leads to less interactive learning due to its lack of flexibility and adaptability.

Level of enjoyment—Similarly, the findings related to how enjoyable learning is when AI is applied and used, participants are split into almost two half-groups; however, more participants (51.1%) believe that learning is more enjoyable with AI than without. The remaining 48.9% believe the opposite is true. This finding supports Hapsari and Wu (2022), who argue that a simple conversation with an AI chatbot boosts learning enjoyment and promotes critical thinking. Similarly, research completed at the University of Idaho (UI) highlighted that students enjoyed interacting with a voice assistant AI tool and asking questions, instead of browsing the internet to search for answers (Terzopoulos & Satratzemi, 2019).

Practicality—Findings demonstrate that 55.3% of the participants identify learning as more practical (experimental) with AI than without. On the other hand, 44.7% consider a less practical learning environment due to AI. This finding supports. Smart Sparrow offers a great number of simulation experiments, such as designing virtual buildings and complex virtual surgeries to allow students to learn by doing. On the other hand, STEVE can show and explain to students how to complete physical and procedural tasks, assist and instruct them.

Personalisation—Level of personalisation is another factor that is impacted by AI tools and systems in higher education institutions in the UK, as discussed previously. Most participants, 61.7%, consider AI to lead to a more personalised learning environment for students, while 38.3% consider the opposite, believing that AI leads to less personalised learning. Teacherbots can provide a personalised teaching experience for students. Students benefit from AI systems implemented to help with their exams and assignments grading process as they receive quicker response and quicker feedback on their results, as well as personalised recommendations based on processing and analysing their answers. Additionally, Palanisamy et al. (2021) discuss that to ensure personalised learning is provided for students, learners' data is continually fed into the systems supported by assessment and real-time feedback.

IT focus—The level of IT-focused learning has been considered as an area highly impacted by AI tools and systems in higher education institutions in the UK. The analysis demonstrates that 93.6% of the participants agree that AI leads to a more IT-focused learning, and only 6.4% of the participants disagree by considering that AI leads to less IT-focused learning. AI supports students by exposing them to technology, and it is vital for their learning, as it assists in developing their technological skills. Moreover, AI provides students with the opportunity to assess the current level of technological skills they have, identify the gaps, and begin developing the skills they are lacking.

Complexity—As with every other technology, AI also brings in a certain level of complexity; therefore, this has been considered as one of the factors impacted by the technology for business postgraduate students and their learning in higher education institutions in the UK. Most of the participants (59.6%) consider AI systems and tools to result in higher levels of complexity for their learning. On the other hand, 40.4% of the participants believe that AI comes with lower complexity levels for students and their learning. Considerable existing research suggests that technological sufficiency and complexity challenges are mostly related to lack of access to technology, technology distributed and accessed unequally, lack of internet access, bandwidth that is too low and slow processing speeds, technical difficulties, and distraction as a result of very complex AI technology.

Feedback—Furthermore, a key impact that AI has on business postgraduate students and their learning is the feedback they receive on their assessments, exams, learning performance, queries, etc. Most of the participants (83%) agree that AI tools and systems allow quicker feedback. These findings align with the existing literature supported by a few researchers. Several AI technologies that utilise ML and natural language processing techniques help students receive evaluations and feedback for different matters while they are studying. The empowerment of AI technologies allows for timely and effective feedback to be provided to students (Hooda et al., 2022).

Cost—New technologies come with a range of costs to implement, and AI is not an exception. The findings from the survey suggest that most of the responses (57.4%) consider AI to allow a lower cost of studying for students; however, quite a high number of participants (42.6%) believe that AI will lead to a higher cost of studying, which consequently might affect learning provision, as it may become difficult to pay for it. These findings align with the existing literature, providing that researchers have considered both the high-cost and low-cost AI for higher education. AI technologies are developing at a very fast pace; however, the cost of this development is quite high due to different factors, such as the availability and format of data, the large amount of data needed, and the infrastructure required to build an AI system or platform. Due to the high costs, universities may increase the fees for students until a low-cost AI is achieved. Furthermore, it will be costly for universities to deploy AI and invest in innovative technologies; on the other hand, in the long term, higher education institutions will experience cost-cutting benefits from AI. Dilmegani (2022) suggests that AI models and platforms are expensive to build; even so, they are cheap to run afterwards. Current researchers agree that initially, AI deployment and application in higher education is costly; however, it will become cheaper in the future, which aligns with the survey findings where participants mainly consider a low-cost AI, but still a high number believe that it is expensive.

Challenge—Challenge of learning new technology, lack of technological competency, intimidation by learning new technology, confusion and resistance about looking for appropriate help online, and difficulty understanding directions and expectations while using AI systems are highlighted as some of the main challenges that AI technologies may bring for students. Quantitative analysis of the survey responses aligns with the existing literature findings and demonstrates that 53.2% of the participants consider AI technologies to make learning more challenging for disabled and vulnerable students; on the other hand, 46.8% consider AI to make learning less challenging for them, especially due to AI's ability to personalise learning.

Independence—Quantitative analysis of the survey data considers independence as an impact that AI has on business postgraduate students' learning. The findings suggest that the majority, 91.5%, of the respondents relate the application of AI tools and systems to a higher level of independence for students and their learning. Similarly, findings from the existing literature analysis suggest that application of AI technologies and systems has made learning more independent, which means that students need to manage their time and organise their learning without being told what and when to do it (Al-Smadi et al., 2025). Similarly, Chaudhary et al. (2024) suggest that the use of AI in higher education allows students to become more engaged and more independent.

Learning performance—Learning performance is the final factor considered as being impacted by AI tools and systems in higher education institutions in the UK. The analysis suggests that 68.1% of the respondents consider an improved student's learning performance due to AI, and 31.9% consider a worsened learning performance due to AI. Similarly, findings from the existing literature suggest that the application of AI in higher education promises significant improvement of business postgraduate students' learning experience with the combination of AI tools and the empowerment of teachers (Schiff, 2021). Furthermore, Hoboken (2020) suggests that the Smart

Sparrow platform offers rich, interactive, and adaptive educational content and a better learning experience for students and better learning outcomes.

Further exploration of the impact of AI on business postgraduate students' learning

To further explore how the applicability and usage of AI in higher education institutions in the UK impacts business postgraduate students' learning, participants were allowed to share their opinion on several questions that consider whether the impact of AI on students' learning is only positive, only negative, equally positive and negative, more positive than negative, with a final overall question that considers how the overall learning experience is impacted by AI. Overall, the findings indicate that most participants either disagreed or remained neutral towards the idea that the impact of AI on students' learning is entirely positive or entirely negative, showing resistance to these extreme positions. Instead, the majority agreed or strongly agreed that AI's influence is both positive and negative in equal measure, with many also agreeing that it is more positive than negative overall. Furthermore, a clear majority agreed that the use of AI tools and systems within higher education improves the learning experience for business postgraduate students, while only a small proportion disagreed or stayed neutral. These findings suggest that participants generally perceive AI as having a beneficial, though balanced, impact on learning—aligning with previous research that highlights AI's potential to enhance education while recognising its limitations compared to human teaching.

Additionally, this section focuses on further correlation analysis and applies Fisher's and Wilcoxon's tests to confirm the results and allow for generalisation. Correlation analysis was completed to investigate participants' views on whether the impact of AI application on business postgraduate students' learning is more positive than negative, as well as whether they consider AI to improve the overall student learning experience. Conducting a correlation analysis between these two aspects enables the researcher to determine whether participants who perceive AI's impact on learning as more positive than negative also believe that AI contributes to improving the overall learning experience. The results suggest a correlation coefficient of 0.497. The coefficient is higher than 0, which demonstrates a medium to strong evidence of a relationship between the responses; specifically suggesting that participants who consider the impact of AI on business postgraduate students' learning to be more positive than negative, also consider that AI would improve the overall learning experience for students. Further analysis using Fisher's and Wilcoxon's tests generates relevant insights.

All aspects related to the impact of AI on learning were compared with participants' views on whether AI improves the overall student learning experience. The results reveal several significant associations. Participants who believed that AI leads to higher-quality learning, quicker feedback, greater complexity, or reduced study costs were also more likely to believe that AI enhances the overall learning experience. A similar association was observed among those who considered AI to improve learning generally. These findings suggest that when participants perceive specific benefits in AI-related aspects of learning, they tend to associate these improvements with a better overall experience. In contrast, for other factors such as interactivity, enjoyment, practicality, personalisation, IT focus, accessibility for disabled students, and independence, no strong statistical association was found, though some results were close to significance. This indicates that while participants often connect AI's positive influence on efficiency, quality, and cost with an enhanced overall learning experience, their opinions are more divided when it comes to AI's role in creating a more interactive, personalised, or inclusive environment. Overall, the findings demonstrate that participants generally view AI as beneficial to learning, but its positive impact appears stronger in practical and outcome-related aspects rather than social or experiential ones.

The Wilcoxon signed rank test was used to determine whether the survey results reflected genuine patterns in opinion or were due to chance, helping to assess if the wider population of business students and academics would share the same views as the study participants. The analysis focused on categorical questions related to perceptions of AI's impact on learning. The comparison of views regarding whether AI's influence is more positive than negative, or vice versa, revealed a clear trend: most participants agreed that AI has a more positive effect on learning, while the majority disagreed that it is more negative. The low p-values obtained from the test (below 0.005) indicate statistically significant results, confirming that these views are unlikely to have occurred by chance and that the wider population would likely share the perception that AI's impact on business postgraduate learning is more positive than negative. Similarly, when examining opinions on whether AI applications in higher education improve the overall student learning experience, the majority of participants agreed that they do. The Wilcoxon test produced a p-value well below the 0.05 threshold, demonstrating a statistically significant result. This finding provides strong evidence that, beyond the sample surveyed, there is a general agreement among the wider population that implementing AI tools in higher education enhances the overall learning experience for business postgraduate students.

Summary

To conclude, the triangulation of findings from the interviews, survey, and existing literature indicates that the impact of AI on business postgraduate students' learning is predominantly positive. Across all three sources, several key benefits were consistently identified, including greater personalisation, flexibility, efficiency, speed, convenience, satisfaction, and self-awareness in learning. These align with much of the existing literature, which highlights AI's ability to enhance learning outcomes, engagement, and accessibility.

Some contradictions were noted, particularly regarding adaptability and cost, with a few studies suggesting that AI systems can still lack flexibility and remain expensive to implement in the short term.

Additional positive themes emerging from the interviews, supported by literature, include improved transparency, accuracy, and access. However, findings on inclusion and fairness were mixed, while interviewees viewed AI as promoting inclusivity, prior research raised concerns about accessibility inequalities and fairness in AI systems.

Negative impacts identified include increased dependence on technology, potential bias, reduced interaction for some learners, and challenges for disabled or vulnerable students. Interestingly, some issues, such as bias and interaction, were perceived differently across methods; for example, interviewees viewed AI as enhancing interaction, while survey respondents saw it as reducing it. These variations are attributed to the mixed-method design and differences in how questions were framed.

Overall, both quantitative and qualitative findings suggest that AI has a more positive than negative impact on business postgraduate students' learning. The Wilcoxon signed rank test confirmed this statistically, indicating strong evidence that the wider population would agree with this view.

Ethical implications of AI tools/systems and their impact on students' learning

Interview analysis and results

This section focuses on exploring the key ethical implications identified from the interview responses and their impact on business postgraduate students' learning. The 15 sub-themes related to the key ethical implications identified include technical implications, confidentiality, cybersecurity, data protection, data security, dependability, inclusion, freedom, loss of human touch, data privacy, transparency, control, bias, awareness, and others.

Technical implications—The analysis demonstrates that the technical implications of AI can lead to ethical implications through three main issues identified from the interviews. AI tools are conditioned to feed repetitive data; otherwise, they cannot function. Feeding data into algorithms is vital for the generation of solutions; nevertheless, it can be very time-consuming, bound to errors and mistakes, and biases; therefore, solutions generated from algorithms are fully dependent on how the data has been inputted.

Confidentiality and cybersecurity—Confidentiality and cybersecurity have been identified by the participants as two types of ethical implications that may occur because of the application of AI tools and systems in higher education institutions in the UK. Akhtar and Rawol (2024) argue that AI can assist the augmentation of cybersecurity; on the other hand, it can likewise assist the augmentation of efforts to bypass security. Moreover, the issue of confidence has been highlighted to understand both how confidential the data that students are providing will be kept, and the confidence level of students that the data will be used ethically.

Data protection, security, and privacy—Further analysis demonstrates that data protection and data security are ethical implications of AI systems applied and used by students in higher education institutions in the UK. Four references identify data protection as an issue, including how data can be misused by third parties. Additionally, nine references identify privacy as a major ethical issue for students and their learning. Consequently, the issue of privacy and security becomes a problem for students. The findings from the analysis also suggest that privacy is the main ethical issue of AI in education, as it is the most repeated sub-theme amongst the responses from the participants.

Dependability and inclusion—Analysis demonstrates that dependability has been identified as not only one of the negative impacts of AI on business postgraduate students' learning but also an ethical implication for students. The automated services that AI provides for students are beneficial; however, they lead to dependence on these systems and therefore a lack of interaction, social skills, and changes in behaviour. According to Buçinca et al. (2025), if our decision-making capacity is turned over to machines, we will become less experienced at making decisions. Furthermore, inclusion has been recognised as an ethical issue for two key reasons: how fair and accessible the systems are for students with disabilities and the inequalities due to limited access in different geographical locations. Technology is distributed and accessed unequally, in several locations, worldwide. There is a lack of internet access, bandwidth that is too low, and slow processing speeds. Consequently, inequalities amongst students in several locations arise, and this leads to ethical issues related to how inclusive these systems can be.

Freedom and loss of human touch—Analysis has identified freedom and loss of human touch as ethical implications that may occur as a result of the use of AI systems by business postgraduate students in higher education institutions in the UK. Identity and freedom within educational settings have started to be questioned due to the ability of AI to manipulate behaviours and decisions. According to Faraoni (2023), AI involves the *use* of information to manipulate behaviour in a way that undermines autonomous rational choice. In addition to freedom, loss of human touch is another ethical issue related to AI systems in education. The teacher's role in higher education institutions is slowly being replaced by AI systems, especially related to automated services such as marking, grading, and feedback; however, intelligent tutoring systems nowadays can replace humans throughout the teaching process. Solutions and services provided to assist students' learning using AI technologies are useful; however, due to these systems being technology-centric and not human-centric, they lack emotions, feelings, interactions, etc. Moreover, AlAfnan et al. (2024) argue that AI is still weak in soft skills such as creativity, innovation, critical thinking, problem-solving, socialising, leadership, empathy, collaboration, and communication.

Transparency, control, bias, and awareness—Further analysis identified four more ethical concerns because of AI tools and systems within higher education institutions: transparency, control, bias, and awareness. Participants argue that there is no transparency around how the data provided will be used and no control over how these data are used or sold. A lack of transparency leads to a lack of understanding of when and how AI is used, which ultimately impacts accountability and puts privacy at risk. Furthermore, findings suggest that AI systems magnify third-degree biases because they are programmed by humans who are inherently biased towards certain language or topics. Humans are the ones who program the algorithms and feed them with repetitive data; therefore, if the data inputted is biased due to unfair judgements by individuals, the outputs generated by the algorithms will automatically be biased. According to Tirado et al. (2024), biases can become an issue even without the intention of the creator of the model; therefore, students in higher education institutions may be subject to biases while using AI and experience several issues. Pazzanese (2020) quotes Michael Sandel, a political philosopher, stating that AI not only replicates human biases, but it also confers on these biases a kind of scientific credibility. It makes it seem that these predictions and judgements have an objective status. AI itself does not decide to do good or bad for the simple reason that it has no ethics; the reason for this is that AI is a technology that is built by humans and therefore basically acts as a mirror to our biases. Finally, awareness has been raised as a matter of ethical concern due to the lack of information students have on what ethical issues they may encounter when using AI in education. De Cremer and Kasparov (2021) state that awareness training should become available to understand ethical concerns of AI, and foremost, to our own good and bad behaviour on how to use AI more responsibly.

Other ethical implications—The final sub-theme identified by the analysis demonstrates three other ethical concerns that did not fit in any of the above 14 sub-themes. The possibility of providing black and white answers to open-ended questions is an implication that can occur when students use AI systems due to their limited ability to respond to complexity. AI systems are as good as the data that has been input to generate solutions. Second, the risk of perpetuating existing problems has been identified as an ethical concern. Findings suggest that if a human lacks certain knowledge in a specific area, or possesses the wrong information, consciously or unconsciously, they feed data to the algorithm based on that knowledge, and the AI system will produce solutions and results that can ultimately be wrong, unfair, and non-inclusive. An example provided explains that if a teacher is preparing slides/content for students and is unaware that the colour contrast is a problem for certain students, when they feed this information to the algorithm, the results produced will lead to some students not being able to read the material that the system has provided.

Finally, analysis shows that ethical implications are not necessarily negative, as everything comes with both advantages and disadvantages. Findings suggest that everything has two sides, advantages and disadvantages, and the only way to overcome the challenges is by first acknowledging them and then understanding them to find a solution. According to De Cremer and Kasparov (2021), technological features that can help data become more transparent and more interpretable should be enhanced, alongside educating human decision-makers in understanding ethical implications that AI can bring, including in higher education institutions in the UK.

Impact of ethical implications

Further analysis explored the impact of ethical implications of AI on learning and four key sub-themes emerged: (1) the first sub-theme considers whether the impact of ethical implications on business postgraduate students' learning is high or low; (2) the second sub-theme considers what type of impact these implications may have; (3) the third sub-theme studies whether it is ethically fair or unfair to not include AI in higher education institutions to avoid ethical implications for students' learning; and (4) the fourth sub-theme discusses whether business postgraduate students have higher or lower level of scepticism in using AI in higher education institutions in the UK when they become aware of the ethical concerns.

High or low impact of ethical implications for learning—With the purpose of understanding the impact of ethical implications on business postgraduate students' learning, it has been noted that it is relevant to explore whether this impact is high or low. Do ethical implications that may occur due to the use and application of AI tools and systems highly impact students' learning in higher education institutions in the UK? To answer this question, the first sub-theme that emerged from the data analysis of the interviews suggests that the impact can be high or low. The findings identify five references that state that the impact is high, and two references that state that the impact is low. The findings suggest that the majority of the responses identify the impact of ethical implications of AI on business postgraduate students' learning as high for several reasons. When ethical concerns arise and students are affected, it may take longer to sort the issues out before students are able to access AI platforms again; therefore, the delays caused may impact the learning. Furthermore, if an AI system/tool makes inaccurate assumptions when responding to questions from a student, or when providing material, content, or suggestions, the student's learning may be highly affected. For instance, if the algorithm has been fed with incorrect information, the tool may suggest to a particular student to study certain material that the student should not study; instead, they may have to revise different content. This could lead to a lower grade in an exam or assignment. Additionally, limited access to platforms has been considered an issue, given that any platforms powered by AI in higher education institutions in the UK operate based on a high level of security, such as password protection, to avoid any ethical concerns raised by a breach of security. Two issues have been identified when accessing the platform;

first, they require the users to log in every time they leave the page, and second, after completing a course, the access to the platform may be limited for security reasons and to avoid ethical issues; therefore, it impacts students' learning. Finally, the findings suggest that AI systems may misinform and mislead students based on the information they provide, which could lead to ethical issues and, therefore, a high impact on learning.

Type of impact—To further understand the impact of ethical implications on business postgraduate students' learning, the analysis generated several types of impacts. The analysis of the interviews identified eight key types of impact that ethical implications of AI may have on business postgraduate students' learning in higher education institutions in the UK. First, it has been noted that the ethical implications of AI cause tension for students and their learning due to the delays they may cause. An example that demonstrates this is when a student has experienced an ethical issue related to a breach of security, and access to a certain platform or account is temporarily denied until the issue is resolved. If the student needs immediate access to the account or platform; however, that is not possible, this will impact their learning and create tension. Moreover, ethical implications may result in reputational impact for students depending on the kind of ethical concern they are experiencing, such as a breach of privacy, data revealed to third parties, or confidential information shared with other students or teachers, etc. Additionally, ethical implications may result in mental health issues for students. Further ways ethical implications impact students' learning have been identified, and the analysis shows that this occurs when AI is misused, when there is a breach of data privacy, and when information has been passed on to third parties in an incorrect way.

Finally, two more types of impact have been recognised; the first one related to biases embedded within the AI systems that could be perpetrated against others, and the second related to issues with learning due to the lack of regulations and awareness of what students consent to. Biases embedded from the use of a specific AI system or tools can easily be perpetuated into other environments and situations and passed on to other individuals. An example identified from the interviews demonstrates that a student who uses VMock, an AI-powered platform that assists students with their CVs, focuses on magnifying the importance of education compared to years of work experience when applying for jobs. If the students are later employed as consultants for a company and assist the company with hiring new employees, they will most likely suggest the company employ people based on their education and not work experience, which may then impact the way the new employees operate in the workplace without having the necessary experience. This shows that biases embedded and learnt from an AI tool can be carried away and can affect decisions and impact people.

Ethically fair or unfair for students' learning to not include AI in higher education institutions in the UK—So far, analysis demonstrated that AI systems, although benefit students' learning, they bring in several ethical implications which can impact the learning highly; thus, it has been considered whether it would be ethically fair or unfair for higher education institutions in the UK to consider not to use any AI tools and systems to support business postgraduate students' learning to avoid ethical implications. Findings suggest that only one participant considers this as fair, and the rest of the participants consider this as unfair for several reasons highlighted as follows. The analysis demonstrates that one reference suggests that it is fair not to include AI in higher education institutions in the UK to avoid ethical implications if there is transparency, if business postgraduate students are aware of this, and they agree to study without having access to the technology. An example of a supermarket where technology is used for express checkout and one that does not have that technology has been provided. If the customer has been made aware that the supermarket has not embraced that technology and they still decide to shop there, that is their choice, and if they know, there is no unfairness.

The rest of the findings suggest that it is ethically unfair not to use AI for business postgraduate students and their learning just to avoid ethical implications. Competitive disadvantage and denial of opportunities and choices have been highlighted as the key sub-themes identified by the majority of the responses. Denying students the opportunity to use AI to support their learning would put them at a competitive disadvantage compared to other students who have access to it. Moreover, living in a world that is moving fast towards embracing technology would leave students disadvantaged and not prepared to face these changes. Additionally, students should always have the options available and make their own choices and decisions. They should be provided with the best possible solutions to embrace cutting-edge technology and decide whether using AI would benefit them and their learning. Considering that the world is moving and changing fast, exposure to technology allows students to get used to it.

Higher or lower level of scepticism in using AI due to ethical issues—To further understand the impact that ethical implications have on business postgraduate students' learning, a final sub-theme has been identified to show whether business postgraduate students have a higher or lower level of scepticism when using AI after they are made aware of the ethical implications that it brings. Eighteen references within 11 files have been identified in the following three categories: higher level of scepticism (17%), lower level of scepticism (72%), and dependent decision (11%). Findings suggest that only 17% of the participants believe that business postgraduate students will feel more sceptical about using AI systems within higher education institutions in the UK when they become aware of what ethical implications they can face as a result. When students try to solve a non-academic issue using the automated systems, they would normally be happy to resolve their issues quickly; however, if students have a more important academic query or concern, they will feel more sceptical about using AI and would prefer human contact rather than talking to a chatbot. Furthermore, it has been noted that students feel more sceptical about using AI within education and their learning than outside in their daily life. Among the responses collected, 72% suggest that even when business postgraduate students become aware of the ethical implications of AI systems that support their learning, their level of scepticism is still low, and they still use the technology. The emergent sub-themes explain the reasons behind this finding, which include transparency, familiarity, risk-taking generation, awareness, etc. Today's generation of students has been considered a risk-taking generation, and no matter what ethical concerns this technology may bring, they still use it to support their learning. The advantages of these technologies outweigh the negative impact they may have on students and their learning; therefore, students' scepticism towards them is lower. Moreover, for some students, especially those who study online or independently and do not have access to face-to-face learning or teachers, they have no other option but to use AI technologies to support their learning, no matter what ethical implications they may bring.

Overall improved or worsened learning experience—The final theme identified from a thorough thematic analysis of the interviews is the overall improved or worsened learning experience as a result of AI in higher education institutions in the UK. This theme supports the analysis. Findings suggest that almost 85% of the participants believe that the use of AI in higher education institutions in the UK improves the learning experience for business postgraduate students, and 15% believe that it could both improve and worsen the experience. No references have been identified that support only a worsened learning experience due to AI. AI in higher education institutions has been considered as a new level of help for business postgraduate students, alongside what is currently available for them to better advance the experience of learning. It is a potential, evolution, and drive for higher education institutions in the UK to adopt AI at multiple levels for both face-to-face and online learning to improve the overall students' learning experience. The technology accelerates learning for students. Previous findings suggest that AI is as good as the information that is embedded within its systems; therefore, as long as resources and time are spent to get AI right from the start, it will improve overall students' learning and experience. This approach leads to potentially reduced human bias, correct information and data fed into the system, a high level of security to protect the data collected, rules and regulations in place to increase awareness and transparency, etc. Furthermore, it has been identified that AI improves the overall business postgraduate students' learning due to facilitation of accessing material and content, the ability of AI to make students' needs visible and support them with personalised solutions and answers in a quicker way, and the supportive nature of AI systems.

Further reasons have been identified that support the overall improvement of business postgraduate students' learning due to the application and use of AI. AI systems incorporated within higher education institutions support students to have access to learning from every corner of the world without the need to travel or be geographically located in the same area as the institution, including those who study independently. Findings suggest that the flexibility that AI offers is one of the key reasons for improved learning and students' experience. In addition, if security issues of AI are addressed through different means, such as a higher level of transparency and awareness, implementation of rules and regulations, getting it right from the start, etc., business postgraduate students' overall learning will improve through the use of AI in higher education institutions in the UK.

Survey analysis and results

To explore the ethical implications of AI on business postgraduate students' learning in higher education institutions, participants were allowed to choose which of the ten options were considered ethical implications of AI. Furthermore, they had the option to list any other ethical concerns that could arise as a result of AI for students and their learning experience.

The findings demonstrate that all the listed options have been selected at least once by the respondents; therefore, considered as ethical implications of AI; however, some have been considered more than others. The list includes the following: the reduction of human contact, privacy, and confidentiality related to personal data, privacy and confidentiality related to data on emotions, competencies, misconceptions, bias and discrimination, lack of personalised learning for disabled and vulnerable students, commercial exploitation of students, lack of transparency, lack of accuracy of data collected, lack of accuracy of non-individual recommendations, and lack of accuracy of predictive recommendations.

Reduction of human contact—The primary ethical implication identified by the participants is the reduction of human contact for students resulting from the use of AI in higher education institutions. The analysis demonstrates that most of the female and male participants consider the human contact to be reduced due to the implementation of AI in higher education institutions in the UK. Similarly, most students and academics/professionals have identified the reduction of human contact as an ethical implication of AI. The existing literature raises this concern by highlighting that the use of AI can restrict students' learning experiences and make them quite different from a typical human experience, based solely on the data that algorithms have been trained on (Haroud & Saqri, 2025). In terms of age, most of the participants in each age group selected this as an ethical implication; however, most of the participants aged 26–29 did not select the reduction of human contact as an ethical implication. Overall, this was the main ethical concern identified by participants; however, it demonstrates that those who did not think of it as an ethical issue mainly belonged to the age group of 26–29, which shows that the younger generation may not consider the lower interaction with humans as an issue. Research suggests that millennials and

Generation Z would prefer to communicate using AI platforms and systems and not humans (Chan & Lee, 2023). Generation Z indicates a higher level of trust in the digital assistants compared to Generation X.

Privacy and confidentiality due to personal data collection—Personal data collection includes the collection of data such as name, date of birth, address, etc., and they are usually collected when students agree to use different applications and websites powered by AI. Alzoubi and Mishra (2025) state that to increase the efficacy and accuracy of AI, there is a need to give up some degree of data privacy. The findings from the survey also suggest that data privacy and confidentiality are amongst the most considered options after the reduction of human contact, as an ethical implication that may result from the implementation of AI in higher education institutions in the UK. The results suggest that the majority of females and all male participants have selected this as an ethical concern. The majority of business postgraduate students and academics/professionals have also considered privacy and confidentiality as an ethical implication of AI. The existing literature also considers privacy a major ethical issue. With AI technologies developing and new features being introduced, privacy related to data collection could be a problem, as it needs constant reviewing and regulating. This may lead to these data being exposed and easily compromising security, privacy, and fairness, which then lead to ethical dilemmas (Dhawan, 2021). In terms of age, similarly, most participants in each age group have considered this an ethical issue. It has been noted that amongst those who have not considered privacy and confidentiality due to the collection of personal data as an ethical concern, the majority belong to the younger age group between 18 and 35, which demonstrates that the younger generation, whether they are students or professionals, are less concerned about the sharing of personal data with AI technology. Research completed by the Global Data and Marketing Alliance in 16 countries across the world (GDMA, 2022) identifies that individuals who belong to the 18–24 age group are the most willing to share their personal data online and are less concerned compared to the older generation. While 76% of the 65+ age group individuals in the UK are concerned about online privacy; the figure drops down to 54% for 18–24s.

Privacy and confidentiality due to collection of students' data on emotions, misconceptions, competencies—Furthermore, privacy and confidentiality because of collection of students' data on emotions, misconceptions, competencies, etc., has also been highly considered as an ethical concern, equally selected by the participants as the privacy and confidentiality due to the collection of personal data. The data analysis suggests that most females, males, students, and academics/professionals have considered this as an ethical implication of AI on students and their learning. Likewise, in terms of age, most of the participants in each age group think of this as an ethical concern. It has been noted that participants over 40 all agree that privacy and confidentiality are ethical concerns. On the contrary, most of the participants who have not selected this to be an ethical issue belong to younger age groups between 18 and 35. Similarly to the previous finding, this demonstrates that the younger generation is less concerned about privacy and confidentiality issues when sharing their data with AI. According to Doyle (2022), the group of individuals called Data Fundamentalists is those individuals who are unwilling to provide personal information. There are 40% Data Fundamentalists in the 65+ age group, but only 9% in the age group 18–24 and 9% in the age group 25–34.

Bias and discrimination—Bias and discrimination have also been considered ethical implications of AI, with an equal selection rate as the previous two concerns. Biases can be created and expressed by algorithms, and it is a natural feature of ML and human understanding. Findings from the survey suggest the same. The majority of females, males, students, and academics/professionals have considered this an ethical concern. In terms of age, the majority of participants from each age group consider bias and discrimination as an ethical issue resulting from the implementation of AI in higher education institutions in the UK.

Lack of personalised learning for disabled and vulnerable students—Although AI attempts to resolve the "one size fits all" learning approach by providing on-demand, customised learning experience, there is little or no evidence that considers personalised learning for disabled and vulnerable students. Few AI tools implemented consider hearing and speaking disabilities; however, vulnerable and disabled students may experience a variety of issues that AI has not yet considered. Furthermore, AI is considered to still be weak in soft skills such as communication, critical thinking, socialising, empathy, etc., which can be crucial skills when dealing with disabled and vulnerable students. The findings from the survey similarly suggest that this has been considered as an ethical concern by 68.1% of the participants overall. Most of all identified groups, graphically, males, females, students, and academics/professionals, have considered it as an ethical concern. Similarly, when divided into age groups, most of the participants from each age group consider the lack of personalised learning for these particular groups of students as an ethical implication of AI in higher education institutions in the UK.

Commercial exploitation of students—Data collected by AI technologies from students can be used externally, by third parties, and for commercial reasons. This can lead to commercial exploitation, especially when it happens without the knowledge and consent of the individuals who provide the data. Of the participants, 53.2% have considered it as an ethical implication due to the use of AI in higher education institutions in the UK; on the other hand, just less than half of the participants do not believe that this can be an ethical concern. In terms of age, only the majority of participants aged 30–35 and over 40s consider this as an ethical concern; the majority in the remaining groups do not identify commercial exploitation as a concern. The findings demonstrate that the majority of the participants who do not believe that commercial exploitation of students is an ethical implication of AI are participants who belong to younger age groups, particularly between 18 and

29. Research completed by Deloitte in 2020 on Digital Consumer Trends suggested that individuals are now more willing to share data with third parties compared to before (Lee & Calugar-Pop, 2020); however, research completed by Statista in 2022 suggests that 21% of the adults in the UK are concerned about their data being shared with third parties, and this is one of the key reasons for concerns (Statista, 2022).

Lack of transparency—Transparency, as another ethical issue of AI, ensures that accountability can be found, and privacy is not at risk by focusing on understanding when and how AI is used. The results from the survey demonstrate that just over half of the participants, 51.1%, identify a lack of transparency as an ethical concern. Almost half of the respondents do not consider it an ethical issue. Amongst those who have selected it as an ethical issue, the majority belong to the male group, academics/professionals, and those aged 30–35 and 36–39. Females are equally split into two groups, whereas most of the students do not consider the lack of transparency as an ethical issue. In terms of age, the majority of younger participants aged between 18 and 29 and older participants aged 40 and above do not consider a lack of transparency as an ethical issue. These findings align with the existing literature, as it also views transparency as an ethical concern; on the other hand, it also considers it as an advantage that AI brings. The example of Jill Watson teacherbot secretly acting as a teaching assistant brings up the issue around transparency of whether learners need to be informed of the fact that they are being taught by AI and not a human. On the other hand, transparency is one of the key strengths of the first generation of AI systems, and the third paradigm of AI, where the learner acts as a leader, is characterised by high levels of transparency (Ouyang & Jiao, 2021).

Lack of accuracy of data collected—In order to train an algorithm, a huge amount of data needs to be used, thus allowing the algorithm to learn, improve, and solve different problems. Consequently, the accuracy of data can become an issue. The findings suggest that only 34% of the participants consider it an ethical issue as a result of AI implementation in the higher education institutions in the UK. Results demonstrate that the majority of the participants consider the lack of accuracy in the data collected not to be an ethical concern for students' learning. This aligns with the findings from the literature, where researchers consider accuracy as one of the advantages of using AI in higher education and for students' learning in particular. According to Alshammari et al. (2025), the strength of AI is its speed, accuracy, and consistency. It is a lost cause to compete with AI on these dimensions.

Lack of accuracy of non-individual recommendations—Based on the information and data used to feed the algorithms, they provide answers, solutions, and recommendations to students' queries and concerns. The analysis aimed to explore whether these algorithms could lead to providing non-individual recommendations that lack accuracy to students. Findings from the survey suggest that only 31.9% of the participants have considered this as an ethical implication of AI for students in higher education institutions in the

UK. The results demonstrate that the majority of males, females, students, and academics/professionals have not identified the lack of accuracy for non-individual recommendations as an ethical concern. The same applies to participants from the majority of different age groups. The findings from this analysis align with what existing literature considers accurate about AI. Yang et al. (2021) argue that AI provides a high level of effectiveness, accuracy, and transparency and assists the learners to achieve augmented intelligence. Furthermore, one of the key strengths of AI is the provision of personalised recommendations and solutions. Students benefit from AI systems implemented to help with their exams and assignments marking process as they receive quicker response and quicker feedback on their results, as well as personalised recommendations based on processing and analysing their answers. Findings from existing literature mainly focus on personalised learning and recommendations for students as a key advantage of AI, like the majority of participants who believe lack of accuracy of non-individual recommendations is not an ethical concern. Like the minority of the participants who believe this to be an ethical concern, a few researchers consider AI to lack the ability to provide personalised solutions and recommendations. Owoc et al. (2021) argue that AI technologies developed and used in higher education institutions provide content and material for several courses; however, although they have been used for a couple of years, they still lack flexibility and adaptability.

Lack of accuracy of predictive recommendations—The analysis aimed to explore whether the algorithms could lead to providing predictive recommendations that lack accuracy for students. Findings from the survey suggest that only 27.7% of the participants have considered this as an ethical implication of AI for students in higher education institutions in the UK. The results demonstrate that the majority of participants in each of the above categories, including males, females, students, academics/professionals, and each age group, have not considered this as an ethical concern as a result of AI implementation in higher education institutions in the UK. Similar to the two previous sections, these findings align with what researchers discuss in the previous research completed. The D2L platform focuses on predicting the right courses for students based on their current progress and development. Furthermore, Xu et al. (2021) discuss that AI aims at developing machines that think like humans and copy human behaviours such as learning, perceiving, predicting, planning, reasoning, etc.

In conclusion, the findings demonstrate that participants believe that the majority of the identified options are ethical concerns that result from the implementation of AI in higher education institutions in the UK. It has been noted that those individuals who have not considered particular options as ethical issues frequently belong to the groups of students and younger generations, given their lack of worry about sharing personal data online compared to older generations (GDMA, 2022) and their preference to communicate using AI platforms and systems, and not humans. These findings contribute to the accomplishment of the second objective of this research by exploring the key ethical implications of AI for students' learning in higher education institutions in the UK. The key ethical concerns include loss of human contact, privacy and confidentiality, bias and discrimination, lack of personalised learning for disabled and vulnerable students, lack of transparency, and commercial exploitation of students.

Impact of ethical implications

To explore how ethical implications brought on by using AI impact students' learning, two main aspects have been considered. Initially, the impact that ethical implications bring for business postgraduate students and their learning has been identified, and second, an analysis was conducted to determine whether they highly impact the learning and students' experience.

To explore the impact of ethical implications of AI on business postgraduate students' learning in higher education institutions in the UK, participants were allowed to choose which of the seven listed answers were considered as an impact that the ethical implications of AI may bring for students and their learning. The results demonstrate that all the available options have been considered as an impact of the ethical implications of AI and have been selected more than once by the participants. It has been noted that all of the responses have been identified as such by more than 50% of the respondents; however, some have been considered more than the others. The available options included reduced quality of learning due to lower human interaction and higher automated systems (78.7%), compromising students' privacy by exploitation of data (66%), monitoring students' activities via personalised learning systems (66%), monitoring students' online conversations (66%), risking students' autonomy using predictive systems (63.8), contributing to racial bias and social discrimination using predictive systems (59.6%), and low accuracy of information and poor learning experiences due to content being produced by algorithms (51.1%).

Reduced quality of learning due to lower human interaction and higher automated systems—As Spera and Agrawal (2025) state, the main focus of AI is to produce automated systems that perform well using any resources, not just humans. This certainly leads to reduced human interaction and higher access to automated systems, consequently leading to ethical issues that impact students' learning. The results demonstrate that most of the participants from each gender group, background group, and age group consider the lowered human interaction to reduce the quality of learning. A minority of business postgraduate students and younger individuals do not believe that less human contact and more automated systems will lead to reduced quality of learning. As stated previously, research suggests that millennials and Generation Z would prefer to communicate using AI platforms and systems, rather than humans.

Compromising students' privacy by exploitation of data—Data exploitation is another ethical issue identified, which can impact students' learning by compromising their privacy. The overall findings suggest that it has been highly considered by the participants as an impact on students' learning; on the other hand, 34% of the respondents do not consider the same. Similarly, as the previous impact considered, most of the participants who have not identified it are students and individuals from the younger age groups between 18 and 35, showing again that younger generations are less concerned about data privacy (GDMA, 2022).

Monitoring students' activities via personalised learning systems—Monitoring students' activities through personalised learning systems benefits students because they receive personalised advice, recommendations, and feedback; however, it can lead to issues with privacy. The majority of the participants consider this to be an impact of ethical implications of AI on business postgraduate students' learning; however, the majority of those who do not belong to the students group, as well as younger age groups between 18 and 35. Similarly as the previous case, the findings suggest that those who do not necessarily think that monitoring of the activities is a concern for students are a considerable number of students and younger individuals.

Monitoring students' online conversations leads to limited participation in learning—If students become aware that, due to the use of AI, their conversations may be monitored, which is an ethical implication of AI as it compromises privacy, students may limit their participation in learning. Of the participants, 66% have considered this as an impact on learning; nonetheless, 34% have not. Almost every category of participants identified consists of a certain percentage of individuals who have not considered this as an impact on students' learning, with the majority being students and participants aged between 26 and 35. Existing literature discusses the monitoring process of AI several times in different research; however, there is no data available that discusses how this impacts students' learning as an ethical concern. STEVE, the intelligent tutoring system focuses on creating a collaborative environment for students by not only demonstrating the tasks but also monitoring the students' performance after the task's completion.

Risking students' autonomy through the use of predictive systems—Arce et al. (2025) argue that AI platforms can predict which courses are suitable for each student to help them make the right choices. This is an advantage for students and their learning; however, predictive systems can increase students' dependency on AI. School systems can become excessively dependent on AI due to the reduction of human presence. Of the respondents, 63.8% believe that predictive systems make students more dependent on AI, thus risking their autonomy.

Contributing to racial bias and social discrimination through automated scoring systems—Owoc et al. (2021) state that students benefit from AI systems implemented to help with their exams and assignments grading process as they receive quicker response and quicker feedback on their results, as well as personalised recommendations based on processing and analysing their answers. An automated marking and scoring system can easily lead to biases and discrimination due to the nature and type of information and data that have been fed into the algorithms from the beginning. AI tools are unable to explain why they make certain choices; planning and attentiveness are vital from the beginning, before harm is created. Similarly, the results from the survey suggest that 59.6% of the participants consider this as an impact of the ethical implications of AI on students' learning. Considering what Professor Jan Willem de Graff (2019) states, that data is always a limited "reflection" (measurement) of a limited part of reality, in essence, it is always biased; it is difficult for humans to avoid biases.

Allowing algorithms to produce content may lead to low accuracy of information and a poor learning experience—Deng (2018) argues that algorithms help machines to solve problems on their own without human guidance. Algorithms operate based on the data and information that is inputted. If the data lacks accuracy, algorithms will automatically produce information, results, solutions, and content that are inaccurate, which could lead to a poor learning experience for students. The findings suggest that just over half of the participants, 51.1%, identified this option as an impact of the ethical implications of AI on students' learning. The results demonstrate that the majority of those who have considered it as an impact on students' learning are females, academics/professionals, and individuals aged between 30 and 35. The majority of males and students, as well as those belonging to 26–29, 36–39, and 50+, do not believe that allowing algorithms to produce content will result in low-accuracy information and a poor learning experience for business postgraduate students. Findings from existing literature correlate with these findings, given that accuracy has both been seen as an advantage of AI and a limitation. AI technologies provide elements of speed and accuracy; however, to increase efficacy and accuracy of AI, there is a need to give up some degree of data privacy. There is no clear relation between the accuracy of information and the impact that it has on learning in the existing literature.

Overall impact

To further explore the impact of ethical implications of AI on business postgraduate students' learning, this section considers: (1) whether the ethical implications of AI highly impact business postgraduate students' learning or not; (2) policies and regulations; (3) whether it is ethically fair or unfair to not include AI in higher education institutions in the UK to avoid ethical implications and their impact; (4) scepticism in using AI after becoming aware of the ethical issues, and (5) overall impact on the learning experience.

High or low impact of ethical implications of AI on students' learning—So far, the analysis has explored the ethical implications of AI and the impact they have on business postgraduate students' learning. On the other hand, it is important to understand whether this impact is high and if it significantly affects learning. The results demonstrate that most of the participants agree that the ethical implications brought on because of AI highly impact business postgraduate students' learning. 46.8% of the respondents agree, and 6.4% strongly agree. Of the participants, 23.4% remain neutral, neither agree nor disagree, 21.3% disagree, and 2.1% strongly disagree. Although there is limited literature related to the impact that ethical implications of AI have on students' learning, particularly, limited research completed supports the survey findings outlined earlier. Porayska-Pomsta et al. (2022) argue that AI in education raises concerns about the significant ethical implications it may have for students and other stakeholders within higher education institutions.

Policies and Regulations—Existing literature suggests that the response from governments and institutions related to ethical implications of AI has been very slow, with only a few recent developments to address these issues (Sun et al., 2024). The Ethical Framework for Artificial Intelligence in Education was created with the purpose of enabling learners to be protected from the risks AI brings, while taking advantage of the benefits of this technology. Although the framework has been updated in 2021, it does not guarantee the framework's fitness for purpose (Buckingham.ac.uk, 2021). Considering the limited regulations and policies within higher education institutions, it has been noted that the ethical implications of AI and the impact that they have on business postgraduate students' learning, but not only, should be carefully identified, and policies and regulations should be put in place by the institutions as well as the governments. The findings from the survey suggest that the majority of the participants agree and strongly agree (36.2% and 44.7%, respectively) that policies and regulations should be considered in order to minimise the impact that AI has on students' learning in higher education institutions in the UK. Existing literature also highlights that there is a lack of policies, procedures, and regulations related to the ethical implications of AI in higher education. The response from governments and institutions related to ethical implications has been very slow, with only a few recent developments to address these issues, even though they have only limited information due to the lack of research. General Data Protection Regulation (GDPR), introduced in the UK in 2018, only covers very limited questions related to the ethical implications of AI in education.

Ethically fair or unfair to not include AI in higher education institutions in the UK to avoid ethical implications—One way to minimise ethical implications and their impact on business postgraduate students' learning is by deciding not to implement AI systems and tools within higher education institutions in the UK. This brings up the question of whether this is ethically fair or not for students, considering that this decision denies students the opportunity to benefit from the advantages of AI. The results demonstrate that participants are almost equally split into two groups, considering this fair and unfair. Of the participants, 25.5% disagree that it is ethically unfair, and 8.5% strongly disagree, which means that they do not believe that it is unfair not to implement AI in higher education just to avoid ethical implications. It has been noted that a significantly high number of participants (27.7%) have remained neutral and unable to say whether that would be ethically fair or unfair. Even so, the majority of participants believe that this would be unfair, as indicated by their agreement and strong agreement with the statement (25.5% and 12.8%, respectively). Existing research comprises a range of peer-reviewed journals and articles that discuss ethical implications and what is ethical and unethical to consider related to AI deployment in higher education. Porayska-Pomsta et al. (2022) argue that it requires significant attention to understand what it means to be ethical when it comes to AI applications in higher education. Moreover, the authors emphasise the importance of distinguishing between doing ethical things and doing things ethically, to make pedagogical choices that are also ethical. Research completed by Kamali et al. (2024) suggests that it is difficult to agree as to what constitutes ethical behaviour; therefore, it is hard to decide whether a decision is ethical or not.

Scepticism—When students' awareness regarding the ethical implications that AI brings for them and their learning increases, they may become more sceptical about using the technology. Participants were asked to consider whether students would have a higher level of scepticism after understanding the ethical issues or not. The findings from the survey suggest that the majority of the participants, 55.3% and 6.4% agree and strongly agree, respectively, that after realising the ethical implications that AI brings for business postgraduate students and their learning, they will become more sceptical in using them. Of the respondents, 14.9% remain neutral, and the remaining 23.4% disagree and strongly disagree. There is no clear evidence in the current literature to explore the level of scepticism in students when becoming more aware of ethical issues of AI; however, research completed by Yampolskiy (2021) suggests that there is a group of individuals who are sceptical towards the risks that AI brings, such as issues related to privacy and discrimination.

Overall impact of ethical implications on students' learning experience—The results indicate that across all four questions, participants generally view the use of AI as beneficial for business postgraduate students' learning, even when ethical implications are considered. Most respondents agreed that students would still have a very positive learning experience from using AI tools despite potential ethical challenges. Only a small group expressed disagreement, while a moderate portion remained neutral. When asked whether AI would lead to a negative learning experience, the majority disagreed, suggesting that they do not see ethical concerns as strong enough to outweigh the educational advantages. Similarly, participants largely agreed that AI contributes more positively to learning than it is hindered by ethical issues. Finally, when asked if ethical implications would significantly harm learning and prevent students from benefiting from AI, most participants disagreed, reinforcing the overall positive view.

In summary, the findings from all four questions show a clear consensus: although participants acknowledge the presence of ethical implications, they believe the educational benefits of AI for postgraduate students far exceed any negative ethical impact.

Further analysis

The correlation analysis explored the relationship between participants' views on the significance of AI's ethical implications and their beliefs about the need for related policies or the overall benefits of AI in learning. The first comparison found only a weak positive correlation between recognising the ethical implications of AI and supporting the implementation of policies and regulations to manage them. This suggests that although many participants agree both that ethical issues are important and that policies are necessary, these views are not always held by the same individuals. In other words, acknowledging the ethical impact of AI on learning does not automatically translate into support for formal policy intervention.

The second comparison examined whether participants who believed that AI's ethical implications have a strong impact on learning also thought that overall learning benefits outweigh these issues. The negative correlation found indicates that participants who viewed ethical concerns as highly significant were less likely to believe that AI's overall benefits surpass its risks. This result aligns with expectations, given the opposing nature of the two perspectives. Overall, these findings suggest that while participants widely recognise both the importance of ethics and the benefits of AI, their views on each are nuanced and not necessarily connected—some focus more on AI's advantages, while others are more cautious about its ethical consequences.

The Wilcoxon signed rank test was used to determine whether the survey results on the ethical implications of AI in learning reflected genuine patterns in opinion rather than random variation, helping to assess whether these views could be generalised to the wider population of business students and academics. The results show mixed but insightful outcomes. When participants were asked whether it would be ethically unfair to avoid AI implementation, responses were highly neutral and evenly split, with no statistically significant result, likely due to confusion over the question. However, significant evidence emerged that most participants believe the ethical implications of AI are meaningful and strongly impact learning, and that policies and regulations should be introduced to minimise ethical risks. These results, supported by very low p-values, suggest that the wider population would similarly agree that managing AI's ethical issues is essential.

Further analysis of questions related to students' experiences and perceptions of AI showed that most participants believe students would become more sceptical towards AI once they understood its ethical implications, while still recognising the positive outcomes of AI use. Statistically significant evidence indicated that the wider population would also agree with this. Moreover, most participants believed that, despite ethical concerns, students would still have a positive learning experience when using AI tools, a finding strongly supported by the Wilcoxon test. Even when questions were framed negatively, suggesting AI could lead to worse outcomes, responses and significance levels indicated weaker support for that view. Finally, the analysis confirmed that the majority agreed AI's benefits to learning outweigh its ethical challenges, with results statistically significant across related questions. Overall, the Wilcoxon analysis demonstrates that the study's findings can be generalised: business postgraduate students and academics in the UK largely believe that while AI raises valid ethical concerns, its overall impact on learning remains substantially positive.

Summary

To summarise, the triangulation of findings reveals that participants, literature, and interviews share a broadly consistent understanding of the ethical implications of AI in higher education, especially in the context of business postgraduate learning. Across sources, several key ethical concerns were identified, including privacy and confidentiality, bias and discrimination, loss of human interaction, dependence on technology, and lack of transparency. Participants in both surveys and interviews acknowledged that AI can raise issues related to data security, accuracy, and inclusivity, particularly for vulnerable students. However, interviews provided more depth, identifying additional ethical dimensions such as technical limitations, freedom of expression, and students' lack of awareness about consent and data use. Literature also complemented these findings, adding accountability and access to technology as further ethical concerns that had not been raised by participants.

Overall, the triangulated analysis suggests that while ethical challenges are significant, they do not negate the potential of AI in education. The combination of data sources shows that participants recognise both the opportunities and risks that come with AI use. Ethical implications such as bias, privacy risks, and diminished human connection are real and need attention through appropriate policies and safeguards. Nevertheless, most findings converge on the view that AI can positively transform learning if its use is transparent, accountable, and inclusive. The research thus presents a nuanced understanding—acknowledging ethical concerns while emphasising the importance of responsible implementation to ensure that AI supports, rather than undermines, student learning and experience.

Conclusion

Overall, the findings indicate that AI has a mostly positive influence on the learning experience of business postgraduate students, particularly in enhancing personalisation, efficiency, feedback, and accessibility. However, the chapter also highlights important challenges, including concerns related to data privacy, reduced human interaction, and increased dependency on technology. While ethical considerations remain significant, the evidence suggests that these issues can be addressed through responsible design, clear regulation, and increased awareness among students and educators. Therefore, the integration of AI into higher education should continue in a balanced and informed manner, ensuring that technological innovation enhances learning without compromising human values or educational fairness.

Reference list

Abogunrin, S., Muir, J. M., Zerbini, C., & Sarri, G. (2025). How much can we save by applying artificial intelligence in evidence synthesis? Results from a pragmatic review to quantify workload efficiencies and cost savings. *Frontiers in Pharmacology*, *16*, 1454245.

Akhtar, Z. B., & Rawol, A. T. (2024). Harnessing artificial intelligence (AI) for cybersecurity: Challenges, opportunities, risks, future directions. *Computing and Artificial Intelligence*, *2*(2), 1485–1485.

AlAfnan, M. A., Dishari, S., & MohdZuki, S. F. (2024). Developing soft skills in the artificial intelligence era: Communication, business writing, and composition skills. *Journal of Artificial Intelligence and Technology*, *4*(4), 305–317.

Al-Badi, A., Khan, A., & Alotaibi, E. (2022). Perceptions of learners and instructors towards artificial intelligence in personalised learning. *Procedia Computer Science*, *201*, C, 445–451.

Ali, M., Wahab, I. A., Huri, H. Z., & Yusoff, M. S. (2025). Personalised learning in higher education for health sciences: A scoping review. *BMC Medical Education*, *25*, 969. https://doi.org/10.1186/s12909-025-07565-1

Alshammari, A. F., Madfa, A. A., Anazi, B. A., Alenezi, Y. E., & Alkurdi, K. A. (2025). Comparison of accuracy and consistency of AI Language models when answering standardised dental MCQs. *BMC Medical Education*, *25*(1), 1507.

Al-Smadi, O. A., Ab Rashid, R., Al-Ramahi, R. A., Alqaryouti, M. H., Ugli, H. S. Z., & Vokhidovich, A. N. (2025). Jordanian English language learners' engagement with AI-supported self-regulated learning. *Research in Learning Technology*, *33*.

Alzoubi, Y. I., & Mishra, A. (2025). Differential privacy and artificial intelligence: Potentials, challenges, and future avenues. *EURASIP Journal on Information Security*, *18*. https://doi.org/10.1186/s13635-025-00203-9

Becker, R. (2022). Gender and survey participation. An event history analysis of the gender effects of survey participation in a probability-based multi-wave panel study with a sequential mixed-mode design. *Methods, Data, Analyses*, *16*(1), 3–32. https://doi.org/10.12758/mda.2021.08

Buçinca, Z., Swaroop, S., Paluch, A. E., Doshi-Velez, F., & Gajos, K. Z. (2025). *Contrastive explanations that anticipate human misconceptions can improve human decision-making skills* (No. arXiv: 2410.04253). arXiv.

Buckingham.ac.uk. (2021). *The institute for ethical AI in education | University of Buckingham*. [online] Retrieved October 30, 2025, from https://www.buckingham.ac.uk/research-the-institute-for-ethical-ai-in-education/

Chan, C. K. Y., & Lee, K. K. W. (2023). The AI generation gap: Are Gen Z students more interested in adopting generative AI such as ChatGPT in teaching and learning than their Gen X and millennial generation teachers?. *Smart Learning Environments*, *10*, 60. https://doi.org/10.1186/s40561-023-00269-3

Chaudhary, A. A., Arif, S., Calimlim, R. F., Khan, S. Z., & Sadia, A. (2024). The impact of ai-powered educational tools on student engagement and learning outcomes at higher education level. *International Journal of Contemporary Issues in Social Sciences*, *3*(2), 2842–2852.

de Cremer, D., & Kasparov, G. (2021). The ethical AI—paradox: Why better technology needs more and not less human responsibility. *AI and Ethics*, *2*(1), 1–4.

de Graff, W. (2019). Sorting machine. *Education Journal*, *378*, 18.

Deng, L. (Eds.). (2018). *Deep learning in natural language processing*. Springer.

Desire2Learn. (2022). *Higher education: Customer success stories*. [online] Retrieved November 13, 2025, from https://www.d2l.com/en-eu/higher-education/customers/

Dhariyal, L. (2021). *MBA in the UK (United Kingdom)—Which are the top 30 MBA colleges in 2021? E-gmat.com*. [online] Retrieved October 29, 2025, from https://e-gmat.com/blogs/mba-uk-united-kingdom/#1-top-30-mba-colleges-in-uk-2021

Dhawan, S. (2021). *Artificial intelligence in higher education: Promises, perils, and perspective*. Expanding Knowledge Horizon. OJAS, *11*, 11–22.

Dilmegani, C. (2022). Advantages of AI according to top practitioners [2022 update]. [online] *AIMultiple*. Retrieved October 10, 2025, from https://research.aimultiple.com/advantages-of-ai/

Doyle, C. (2022). *UK consumers less concerned about data privacy*. Research Live. [online] Retrieved October 29, 2025, from https://www.research-live.com/article/news/uk-consumers-less-concerned-about-data-privacy-/id/5097032

Faraoni, S. (2023). Persuasive technology and computational manipulation: Hypernudging out of mental self-determination. *Frontiers in Artificial Intelligence*, *6*, 1216340.

Farhan, N. D., Sadiq, B. H., Zwayyer, M. H., & Arnout, B. A. (2024). The impact of using artificial intelligence techniques in improving the quality of educational services/case study at the University of Baghdad. In *Frontiers in education* (Vol. 9, p. 1474370). Frontiers Media SA.

Global Data and Marketing Alliance (GDMA). (2022). *Global data privacy: What the consumer really thinks*. [online] Retrieved October 29, 2025, from https://globaldma.com/association/consumers-across-the-globe-are-increasingly-comfortable-sharing-their-data/

Goenka, N., Choudhury, T., & Ahuja, N. J. (2021). Enhancing number sense of dyscalculia learners by pedagogical agents: A review. *Emerging Technologies in Data Mining and Information Security: Proceedings of IEMIS 2020*, Volume 1, 827–839.

Han, B. (2017). Research on independent learning mode under the background of internet plus. In *Proceedings of the 2nd international conference on contemporary education, social sciences and humanities*. ICCESSH. https://doi.org/10.2991/iccessh-17.2017.65

Hapsari, I. P., & Wu, T. T. (2022). AI chatbots learning model in English speaking skill: Alleviating speaking anxiety, boosting enjoyment, and fostering critical thinking. In *International Conference on Innovative Technologies and Learning* (pp. 444–453). Springer.

Haroud, S., & Saqri, N. (2025). Generative AI in higher education: Teachers' and students' perspectives on support, replacement, and digital literacy. *Education Sciences*, *15*(4), 396. https://doi.org/10.3390/educsci15040396

Hattie, J. (2019). *Visible Learningplus 250+ influences on student achievement*. Corwin. Retrieved November 9, 2025, from https://visible-learning.org/wp-content/uploads/2018/03/VLPLUS-252-Influences-Hattie-ranking-DEC–2017.pdf

Higher Education Statistics Agency (HESA). (2022). *Where do HE students come from?* [online] Retrieved October 29, 2025, from https://www.hesa.ac.uk/data-and-analysis/students/where-from

Hoboken, N. (2020). *Pearson acquires interactive learning technology from smart sparrow*. [online] Prnewswire.com. Retrieved October 9, 2025, from https://www.

prnewswire.com/news-releases/pearson-acquires-interactive-learning-technology-from-smart-sparrow–300987673.html

Hooda, M., Rana, C., Dahiya, O., Rizwan, A., & Hossain, M. (2022). Artificial intelligence for assessment and feedback to enhance student success in higher education. *Mathematical Problems in Engineering*, *2022*, 1–19.

Kamali, J., Paknejad, A., & Poorghorban, A. (2024). Exploring the challenges and affordances of integrating ChatGPT into language classrooms from teachers' points of view: An ecological perspective. *Journal of Applied Learning and Teaching*, *7*(2), 168–180.

Kuhail, M. A., Alturki, N., Thomas, J., & Alkhalifa, A. K. (2024). Human vs. AI counseling: College students' perspectives. *Computers in Human Behavior Reports*, *16*, 100534.

Le Dinh, T., Le, T. D., Uwizeyemungu, S., & Pelletier, C. (2025). Human-centered artificial intelligence in higher education: A framework for systematic literature reviews. *Information*, *16*(3), 240. https://doi.org/10.3390/info16030240

Lee, P., & Calugar-Pop, C. (2020). *Changing attitudes to data privacy*. Deloitte. [online]. Retrieved October 29, 2025, from https://www2.deloitte.com/uk/en/pages/technology-media-and-telecommunications/articles/digital-consumer-trends-data-privacy.html

Mulder, J., & de Bruijne, M. (2019). Willingness of online respondents to participate in alternative modes of data collection. *Survey Practice*, *12*(1). https://doi.org/10.29115/SP-2019-0001

Naibaho, L. (2019). The effectiveness of independent learning method on students' speaking achievement at Christian University of Indonesia Jakarta. *Asian EFL Journal Research Articles*, *23*(6.3).

NSW Education. (2020). *Learning modes*. [online] Retrieved October 9, 2025, from https://education.nsw.gov.au/teaching-and-learning/school-learning-environments-and-change/future-focused-learning-and-teaching/learning-modes

Ouyang, F., & Jiao, P. (2021). Artificial intelligence in education: The three paradigms. *Computers and Education: Artificial Intelligence*, 2, 100020.

Owoc, M., Sawicka, A., & Weichbroth, P. (2021). *Artificial intelligence technologies in education: Benefits, challenges and strategies of implementation*. http://www.ue.wroc.pl/en/.

Palanisamy, P., Thilarajah, S., & Chen, Z. (2021). Providing equitable education through personalised adaptive learning and assessment. In *Back to the future—ASCILITE*. ASCILITE Publications, pp. 202–207.

Pangaribuan, B., Purba, N., Siahaan, K., Sidabutar, E., Sihombing, V., Simamora, D., & Matondang, J. (2022). The implementation of demonstration method to increase learning outcome in natural science lessons. *Jurnal Obsesi: Jurnal Pendidikan Anak Usia Dini*, *6*(4), 3680–3692.

Pazzanese, C. (2020). Ethical concerns mount as AI takes bigger decision-making role in most industries. *The Harvard Gazette*. Retrieved November 8, 2025, from https://news.harvard.edu/gazette/story/2020/10/ethical-concerns-mount-as-ai-takes-bigger-decision-making-role/

Porayska-Pomsta, K., Holmes, W., Holstein, K., Sutherland, E., Baker, T., Shum, S. B., Santos, O. C., Rodrigo, M. T., Cukurova, M., Bittencourt, I. I., & Koedinger, K. R. (2022). Ethics of AI in education: Towards a community-wide framework. *International Journal of Artificial Intelligence in Education*, *32*, 504–526. https://doi.org/10.1007/s40593-021-00239-1

Remian, D. (2019). Augmenting education: Ethical considerations for incorporating artificial intelligence in education. *Instructional Design Capstones Connection*. https://scholarworks.umb.edu/instruction_capstone/52

Saputra, R., Hambali, I., Muslihati, M., Setiyowati, A. J., Lidyawati, Y., & Situmorang, D. D. B. (2024). The metamorphosis of education: An opinion on how artificial intelligence is changing education. *Journal of Public Health*, *46*(1), e165–e166.

Schiff, D. (2021). Out of the laboratory and into the classroom: The future of artificial intelligence in education. *AI & Society*, *36*, 331–348. https://doi.org/10.1007/s00146-020-01033-8

Singh, V., & Thurman, A. (2019). How many ways can we define online learning? A systematic literature review of definitions of online learning (1988–2018). *American Journal of Distance Education*, *33*(4), 289–306.

Slauson-Blevins, K., & Johnson, K. M. (2016). Doing gender, doing survey? Women's gatekeeping and men's non-participation in multi-actor reproductive surveys. *Sociological Inquiry*, *86*(3), 427–449.

Smart Sparrow. (2022). *About Smart Sparrow*. [online] Retrieved November 9, 2025, from https://www.smartsparrow.com/about/

Spera, C., & Agrawal, G. (2025). *Reversing the paradigm: Building AI-first systems with human guidance*. arXiv preprint arXiv:2506.12245

Squirrel AI. (2022). *Our development and milestones*. [online] Retrieved October 13, 2025, from http://squirrelai.com/our-development-and-milestones

Statista. (2022). Thinking about the protection of your personal information, what would you say are your concerns? *Statista*. [online] Retrieved October 29, 2025, from https://www.statista.com/statistics/1184872/concerns-about-personal-data-protection-uk/

Sun, N., Miao, Y., Jiang, H., Ding, M., & Zhang, J. (2024). *From principles to practice: A deep dive into AI ethics and regulations*. arXiv preprint arXiv:2412.04683

Tahir, M., Hassan, F. D., & Shagoo, M. R. (2024). Role of artificial intelligence in education: A conceptual review. *World Journal of Advanced Research and Reviews*, *22*(1), 1469–1475.

Terzopoulos, G., & Satratzemi, M. (2019). Voice assistants and artificial intelligence in education. In *Proceedings of the 9th Balkan Conference on Informatics* (pp. 1–6). ACM Digital Library.

Tirado, A. M., Mulholland, P., & Fernandez, M. (2024). *Towards an operational responsible AI framework for learning analytics in higher education*. arXiv preprint arXiv:2410.05827

UNESCO. (2020). *Global education monitoring report 2020: Inclusion and education: All means all*. 92310038.

Wan, T. (2020). *Pearson bets on adaptive learning (Again) With $25M acquisition of Smart Sparrow*. [online] EdSurge. Retrieved October 9, 2025, from https://www.edsurge.com/news/2020-01-22-pearson-bets-on-adaptive-learning-again-with-25m-acquisition-of-smart-sparrow

Williams, S. (2008). *Does gender influence online survey participation. A record linkage analysis of University Faculty online survey response behavior*. https://eric.ed.gov

Xu, L. D., Lu, Y., & Li, L. (2021). Embedding blockchain technology into IoT for security: A survey. *IEEE Internet of Things Journal Early Access*. https://doi.org/10.1109/JIOT.2021.3060508

Yampolskiy, R. V. (2021). *AI risk skepticism*. arXiv preprint arXiv:2105.02704

Yang, S. J., Ogata, H., Matsui, T., & Chen, N. S. (2021). Human-centered artificial intelligence in education: Seeing the invisible through the visible. *Computers & Education: Artificial Intelligence*, 2, Article 100008.

Zhao, Y., & Liu, G. (2019). How do teachers face educational changes in artificial intelligence era. In *Proceedings of the 2018 International Workshop on Education Reform and Social Sciences (ERSS 2018)*. https://doi.org/10.2991/erss-18.2019.9

7 Rethinking the future of AI in higher education

Institutional strategies for responsible adoption of AI

Introduction

AI is increasingly reshaping higher education, offering new possibilities for personalised learning, flexible study pathways, and enhanced academic support. While AI has been present in educational contexts for several decades, recent technological advances and wider accessibility have accelerated its integration into teaching, learning, and curriculum design. In the context of business postgraduate education, AI tools such as intelligent tutoring systems, adaptive platforms, and automated feedback mechanisms are beginning to influence how students engage with knowledge, how educators design learning experiences, and how institutions deliver support. At the same time, the growing presence of AI raises important questions regarding data privacy, ethical responsibility, reliance on technology, and the evolving role of the teacher. This chapter explores the future direction of AI in higher education, examining its potential to transform learning experiences while recognising the challenges and considerations that must be addressed to ensure its use remains equitable, ethical, and student-centred.

The future of AI

AI applied and used in higher education institutions is at present a reality with beneficial results already obtained; however, it is only a marginal reality as it has not been developed sufficiently or applied widely (Shahzad et al., 2024). Although AI has been present in higher education for a few decades, its prospects and usage are now greater than before due to certain reasons, such as the wider access to the internet and computers and the advances in research; therefore, it can be argued that AI is leaving the laboratory and entering the classroom (Crompton & Burke, 2023). Founder of Squirrel AI, one of the AI tools already used in universities, Derek Li, argues that AI adaptive systems can produce miracles, and entrusting teachers may risk damaging geniuses (Hao, 2019).

Amiri (2025) argues that AI will encourage policymakers and experts in higher education institutions to concentrate on a totally innovative paradigm

DOI: 10.4324/9781003664161-7

with a greater emphasis on inspiration, imagination, and civic engagement. Curricula, as another aspect of higher education, will be significantly affected by AI. Jaramillo and Chiappe (2024) argue that as new and better AI-based applications are developed and applied in higher education, the curricula will become more and more flexible and adaptable. AI technologies will also significantly change the way students find, accumulate, and interact with information. Besides, these technologies will significantly affect the ability of students to use trial-and-error methods to reduce fear from learning and learn in an environment with almost no rules, where AI teachers suggest answers to improve (Aldosari, 2020). AI tools will be able to make available thorough data related to students' learning, allow exceptional levels of diversity, and augment the status of the profession.

New paradigm

Murniarti and Siahaan (2025) argue that AI will encourage policymakers and experts in higher education institutions to concentrate in a totally innovative paradigm with a greater emphasis on inspiration, imagination, and civic engagement; and AI will be able to fully adapt material and information to students' needs and provide feedback and encouragement because of its capacity to monitor participation, guide learning, and engage students. Arar and Chen (2021) argue that higher education should focus on the development of a new paradigm, given that the need for learning, education, and knowledge to be reimagined is increasing, considering the rapidly changing, complex, and uncertain world we live in. Consequently, AI can help the development of the new paradigm to shape the future and implement appropriate institutional transformation. AI-based tools promise a significant qualitative enhancement in higher education due to the ability to provide students with customised learning and to achieve a better integration between humans and face-to-face learning with the new AI technologies.

Curricula

Curricula are another aspect of higher education that will be significantly affected by AI. Chu and Ashraf (2025) argue that as new and better AI-based applications are developed and applied in higher education, the curricula will become more and more flexible and adaptable to all the new ways of understanding educational tasks in the years to come. Jaramillo and Chiappe (2024) also focus on the effect that AI will have on the curricula. They argue that the reason behind that is the fact that AI technologies provide elements of speed and accuracy. The historical aim of universities has always been to be able to take any subject material and make it available to everyone, everywhere, at any time. This has not fully been achieved with Massive Open Online Courses (MOOCs); however, with the help of AI technologies, it could lead to the universalisation of the curricula as well as addressing any previous educational quality issues (Schiff, 2021). MOOCs are offered in a large number of universities across the world, including Harvard University, Stanford University, MIT (Massachusetts Institute of Technology), Berkeley University in the USA, University of Birmingham, University of York, University of Southampton, and University of Glasgow, etc. in the UK (MOOC Courses, 2022). Shah et al. (2022) list many MOOC platforms powered by AI and used worldwide, including: Coursera in the USA, Future Learn in the UK, France Universite Numerique in France, Miriadax in Spain, EduOpen in Italy, OpenHPI in Germany, SWAYAM in India, Fisdom in Japan, Edraak in Jordan, XuetangXi in China, and many more. The universalisation of curricula using AI can be a challenge due to the nature of the technology. Providing that mathematics is a science that relies on standard equations and problem-solving procedures, it is easier for AI to model it; however, on the other hand, understanding meaning and context is far more challenging for the technology (bin Mohamed et al., 2022).

Feedback

Deepshikha (2025) lists several ways in which AI is expected to be applied in the future and impact higher education. AI technologies will likely be able to fully automate the classification and grading system in universities and enable students to obtain a lot more support than they currently have. Furthermore, students and teachers will have the opportunity to share feedback and comments more efficiently and effectively, thus benefiting from shared experiences. Faulconer et al. (2021) argue that feedback is important for students as it provides insights related to their performance and their strengths and weaknesses. The empowerment of AI technologies allows for timely and effective feedback to be provided to students, which is crucial for several reasons, such as (1) increased academic performance, (2) self-regulated learning, (3) increased student motivation, (4) enhanced student engagement, and (5) addressed accountability issues (Hooda et al., 2022).

Information and improvement

AI technologies will also significantly change the way students find, accumulate, and interact with information. This has already impacted the way information is being searched and accumulated; however, with the development of new AI-based technologies, it will become more substantial (Al Mashagbeh et al., 2025). The authors' study found that 89% of students across 27 universities in Jordan reported using AI tools for academic tasks, and 86.6% perceived them as educationally beneficial. Appedu (2022) also argues that the future of information seeking is increasingly being shaped by AI. Furthermore, AI systems will considerably affect how students progress in their study courses by indicating which areas they need to improve and ensuring that all students form the same theoretical fundamentals by receiving instant feedback and advice, without the need to wait for the teacher. AI machines help to accelerate data understanding and management, which leads to improved decision-making and learning processes.

Fear of learning and location

Besides, AI-based technologies will significantly affect the ability of students to use trial-and-error methods to reduce fear from learning and learn in an environment with almost no rules, where AI teachers suggest answers to improve (Villegas-Ch et al., 2025). AI systems will be able to change students' learning location, the style of gaining skills, and who teaches them by allowing them to choose the proper places for learning, whether at home, at the university, or just at a coffee shop. Lopez-Gazpio (2025) suggests that AI will allow students to access global classrooms no matter where they are located or whether they speak a different language or are simply ill and cannot attend a physical lesson.

Increased level of understanding

Salloum et al. (2025) also focus their research on the future impact of AI systems and their applicability in higher education, and more specifically on students' learning. The authors argue that AI systems will be able to deeply understand students, including their cognitive development and history, emotional reactions, level of engagement, and even their future educational pathways. Similarly, Nunes and Antunes (2024) argue that in the future, AI machines will be capable of understanding human language, including everything that is spoken and written.

Teachers

Chan and Tsi (2023) argue that a very important role of AI systems in the future will be to empower teachers so that students are provided with a better learning experience. The author states that many AI-based tools cannot function without the presence of teachers and are designed to coordinate with them rather than replace them. Elstad (2024) also argues that AI systems are there to support and enhance rather than displace teachers. AI systems will be able to free teachers from the most repetitive tasks and allow them to focus on supporting students with their professional development, educational goals, their careers, etc. (Ruziev, 2025). AI tools will be able to make available thorough data related to student learning, allow exceptional levels of diversity, and augment the status of the profession. The future of AI promises significant improvement of students' learning experience with the combination of AI tools and the empowerment of teachers; however, the role of teachers in the future has already started to be questioned. Sparrow and Flenady (2025) discuss the worrying possibility of teaching being replaced by

AI, which could be profitable in the long run but is just a superficial approach. They argue that careful consideration should be given to the enticement to consider education equal to the resolutions provided by algorithms, where they fully replace the human mind.

Educational ownership

Finally, Navas Bomilla et al. (2025) discuss the fact that AI will provide students with what is called educational ownership, where students fully control their destiny in terms of education. They will be able to choose their own courses, study at their own pace, and anticipate their academic and professional path. Educational ownership will then become an increasingly local project where students and their families, as well as their teachers, will engage in enhanced educational, societal, and public outcomes. Similarly, Peng and Li (2025) consider that educational ownership is about students being self-directed, engaged, and motivated, and able to direct and design their own learning experience.

Major contributions of the research

Theoretical contribution

Secondary data research from peer-reviewed journals, articles, books, and news sites highlighted little research completed on the impact that AI has on students' learning. Data available is essentially related to the impact that AI has on education in general, and research has been completed in several countries around the world. The secondary data that described the impact of AI were focused on three aspects within higher education institutions: learning, teaching, and administration. Several challenges and benefits of AI on students' learning were identified through the existing literature; however, the data was limited, and there was no evidence of research completed for higher education institutions in the UK, particularly. Secondary research allowed the identification of the key learning modes for students; however, there was no research conducted about which AI tool and system would best suit each of the learning modes. Therefore, the first theoretical contribution consists of AI tools and systems identified for each of the five key learning modes: face-to-face (explicit), online, independent, demonstration, and feedback and reflection. The findings from this research confirmed that several AI tools and systems are applicable for each learning mode, some to be applied in more than one, and several others are considered suitable for just one particular mode of research. The findings also suggest that the most considered technologies include tools and systems that provide feedback, chatbots for general queries, platforms for content, material, tests, and intelligent tutoring systems. The highest number of tools considered to add value and support students' learning are identified for the face-to-face (explicit) and online learning modes.

Furthermore, as mentioned earlier, several benefits and disadvantages of AI on students' learning were identified through literature; however, there was little research completed for higher education institutions in the UK particularly; therefore, the second contribution to the literature consists of the impact that these AI tools and systems have on business postgraduate students' learning in higher education institutions in the UK only. The findings of this research suggest that the impact is mainly positive, and it is mainly related to accessibility, personalisation, flexibility, efficiency, speed, inclusion, transparency, accuracy, quality, independence, etc. On the other hand, the negative impact of AI tools and systems has been identified; however, the negative impact is smaller than the positive impact. The negative impact mainly consists of bias, memory, dependability, superficial technologies, cost, complexity, and challenging systems for disabled and vulnerable students.

Ethical concerns brought on by the use of AI tools in higher education institutions are a major issue for which very limited research has been conducted, and insufficient guidelines and policies have been created by institutions, organisations, and governments. Secondary data research from peer-reviewed journals, articles, books, news sites, and websites generated limited information on some of the ethical implications of AI for students and how they affect their learning; nevertheless, the data generated is incomplete. Furthermore, the research completed so far on the ethical implications of AI was particularly focused on the ethical concerns for education in general, and there was very little evidence of how these issues impact students' learning. Therefore, the third theoretical contribution of this research consists of an understanding of the key ethical implications of AI and how they impact business postgraduate students' learning in higher education institutions in the UK. The findings of this research suggest that several ethical implications of AI have been identified, including technical implications, confidentiality, data privacy and security, data protection, dependability, inclusion, freedom, loss of human touch, transparency, control, bias, awareness, accuracy, and accountability. The findings further identify that the impact of ethical implications of AI on students' learning is high due to several reasons: delays they may cause for the learning, issues with accessibility, misinformation, tension, reputational impact, mental health issues, reduced quality and performance of learning, students missing out on education, etc.

Linking the current theories of AI and learning discussed in the literature review section of the thesis with the research, there are some interesting contributions identified. One of the key findings of the research suggests that there are several ethical implications for business postgraduate students and their learning due to the application of AI in higher education institutions. Key issues identified are mainly related to control, privacy, freedom, and awareness. Considering the AI paradigms and learning theories previously discussed, if higher education institutions in the UK follow an AI-directed approach with the learner as recipient, they will allow the technology to direct students' choices, learning, and pathways, in the same way as behaviourism would leave students with no choice of the learning path. This would negatively contribute to the ethical implications identified, as it would increase the level of control and contribute to less freedom. Students will have fewer choices, and that would lead to more issues with privacy and decreased awareness. To minimise the risk of ethical implications and their impact on students' learning, higher education institutions in the UK should focus on AI-supported and AI-empowered paradigms where learners have more freedom and control over their choices. Learners would be able to identify the key technologies that would work best for them, leading to an increased level of awareness, potentially reduced privacy issues, and overall, a higher level of effectiveness, accuracy, and transparency to achieve augmented intelligence. Furthermore, if learners act as leaders, they can manage the risks of automated AI decisions.

Another key finding of this research focuses on the identification of the key AI tools that are most applicable for each learning mode. The most important tools discussed include technologies related to providing feedback, content and material, chatbots, and tools that are inclusive of all, no matter what their disabilities are. Similarly, as above, if higher education institutions focus on an AI-directed approach, learners would not be able to choose their path and learning tools; thus, they could be required to learn through platforms that may not be suitable for their skills, abilities, and knowledge. This could result in receiving feedback that is not appropriate to the expectations of students and their learning development. On the other hand, if students can construct their own meaning of the material and content and utilise AI tools to build mutual and active interactions and personalised learning experience through AI-supported and empowered paradigms, they can make their own choices of platforms, other tools, that is, chatbots, including those which would be inclusive of their needs.

Furthermore, this research considers the negative impact that the application of AI tools brings to business postgraduate students and their learning. Some of the key issues identified in terms of the negative impact include inherited biases of the tools, impact on memory due to dependence on AI, digital illiteracy, and challenges for disabled students. To overcome these challenges, higher education institutions would benefit from AI-supported and AI-empowered paradigms for several reasons. First, this would allow students to take ownership of their learning and only use AI technologies for support and to achieve augmented intelligence; thus, avoiding issues with memory and dependence on AI. An AI-directed approach could lead to more dependency on the technology. Second, an AI-directed approach would not consider students' issues with illiteracy and disabilities, due to its nature to control their choices. On the other hand, an AI-supported and AI-empowered approach allows for more flexibility for students to make their own choices, consider tools and materials they are comfortable with and able to use, and make decisions related to AI and their learning.

Finally, the research identified that personalised learning is one of the key benefits of AI tools for business postgraduate students' learning. Contrary to AI-supported and AI-empowered paradigms, the AI-directed paradigm defines the learning goals, content, and procedures, and only some systems collect information about students to understand their learning state. This would hinder their ability to receive personalised learning advice, feedback, content, and material. On the other hand, an AI-supported paradigm allows the collection of individualised information for learners and uses it as an input to adapt the learning and provide an individualised learning experience. Similarly, an AI-empowered paradigm focuses on learners achieving a more efficient and personalised learning experience.

The preceding analysis shows that there is a clear link between AI paradigms, learning theories, and the research completed. AI in education has moved from paradigm one (AI-directed) to paradigm two (AI-supported), and it is currently moving to the third paradigm (AI-empowered). This is well-supported in this research, which clearly identifies that the focus should be on personalised learning, minimising the negative impact of AI on learning, and the risk of ethical implications through a more collaborative approach where the learners are responsible for their learning, and AI is available to augment their experience and personalise it.

Overall, the research findings contribute to the theory by identifying that the impact of AI tools and systems on business postgraduate students' learning in higher education institutions in the UK is more positive than negative and leads to an improved learning experience. This finding is supported by the existing research. AI machines help to accelerate data understanding and management, which leads to improved decision-making and learning processes. The future of AI promises significant improvement of students' learning experience with the combination of AI tools and the empowerment of teachers.

Research limitations

This research is innovative, and its contribution is significant towards understanding and exploring the impact of AI on business postgraduate students' learning, particularly in higher education institutions in the UK. To the best of the researcher's knowledge, this is a contemporary phenomenon that is currently affecting education and higher education institutions in the UK, particularly; therefore, it is expected to add value to the existing literature and to higher education institutions in the UK. Even so, the research has its own limitations, similar to all other studies.

This research focused on exploring and further examining the impact of AI on business postgraduate students' learning in higher education institutions in the UK, only considering the gap in the literature and very limited or no research completed for this topic in these particular institutions. If the research had been completed for other higher education institutions, outside of the UK, it would have provided different perspectives and views from the participants, and it would have allowed wider findings; however, this was not considered due to the key focus of the research being the institutions in the UK. The findings can be easily generalised for higher education institutions inside the UK; however, the generalisation for higher education institutions in other countries, where the culture and context are different, needs to be considered with caution. Nevertheless, the approach used to generate these findings can be adapted to a variety of situations, thus allowing external validity examination. Finally, the research was limited to MBA students and MBA academics/professionals only, given that postgraduate level students are more mature and have had more opportunities to be exposed to AI technologies and tools in education, in their undergraduate and postgraduate studies. This allowed for a better understanding of the topic, given that not everyone is aware of what AI is and how it can impact students and their learning.

Recommendations

Recommendations for future research

This research highlights the impact of AI on students' learning in higher education institutions in the UK by exploring the key AI technologies applicable for business postgraduate students in the different learning modes of research and the impact they have on learning. Furthermore, it explored the ethical implications of AI and the impact they have on learning. The findings suggested that even though several negative impacts of AI technologies and ethical implications have been identified, the overall impact is positive and allows for an improved learning experience. Considering these findings and the limitations of the research discussed earlier, it is recommended that further comparative research within higher education institutions in the UK and higher education institutions outside of the UK is completed to further validate the findings. Additionally, further research should be completed to explore what policies and procedures, alongside rules and regulations, higher education institutions in the UK should implement to minimise the risks of ethical implications that AI brings for students and their learning.

Practical implications: recommendations for higher education institutions in the UK

The opportunity to collect data through three different sources, existing literature, semi-structured interviews, and surveys, allowed a better understanding of what impact AI can have on business postgraduate students and, to some extent, how this impact can be minimised when it is negative. The following are several recommendations for higher education institutions in the

UK to implement when considering the application and usage of AI systems to support students' learning:

1. Ensure AI systems and tools are inclusive of all groups of students, including those who are vulnerable and disabled.
2. Given that higher education institutions in the UK provide online courses and enrol students who live internationally, they should implement procedures to support those students who have less access to technology and broadband to avoid them missing out on education.
3. Given the considerable number of ethical issues that AI can bring and the high impact they have on students' learning, higher education institutions in the UK should start developing policies and procedures and follow strict rules and regulations when implementing AI systems to minimise the risk of ethical issues for students.
4. Higher education institutions in the UK can introduce courses and training for students, related to the AI systems and ethical issues they may encounter when using them, to increase students' awareness and minimise the risk of the negative impact of the ethical concerns.
5. Consent forms and terms and conditions that students sign when providing personal data while using AI technologies can be easier to understand and shorter, for students to read them before signing. This increases awareness and informs students about any expected risks.
6. AI is still in the process of developing and changing very fast; therefore, systems that are unexplainable, hard to understand, use, and apply should be avoided until these changes are made, to avoid any ethical concerns and negative impact on students and their learning.
7. Finally, any AI system implementation should go alongside policies and procedures and applicability in higher education institutions to increase awareness, transparency, and minimise negative impact.

Conclusion

The future of AI in higher education promises substantial improvements in student learning experiences, curriculum flexibility, and teaching effectiveness. AI-based systems have the capacity to provide personalised guidance, facilitate real-time feedback, and support educational ownership, allowing students to shape their own learning trajectories. While the technology can streamline administrative and repetitive tasks, its optimal application requires collaboration with teachers, who remain central to mentorship, professional development, and human-centred pedagogy. The findings underscore that AI should empower and support students and educators rather than replace them. Furthermore, ethical considerations, including privacy, inclusivity, transparency, and bias, must be addressed to ensure responsible implementation. By adopting AI-supported and AI-empowered paradigms, higher education institutions can enhance learning outcomes, foster student autonomy, and prepare graduates for increasingly complex and dynamic global environments. Future research and institutional policies should continue to refine the integration of AI in education, balancing technological innovation with pedagogical integrity and ethical responsibility.

Reference list

Al Mashagbeh, M., Alsharqawi, M., Tudevdagva, U., & Khasawneh, H. (2025). Student engagement with artificial intelligence tools in academia: A survey of Jordanian universities. In *Frontiers in education* (Vol. 10, p. 1550147). Frontiers.

Aldosari, S. (2020). The future of higher education in the light of artificial intelligence transformations. *International Journal of Higher Education*, *9*(3), 145–150.

Amiri, S. M. H. (2025). *The role of artificial intelligence in shaping future education policies*. SSRN: 5193088.

Appedu, S. (2022). *AI infodemic: Interrogating algorithms of information seeking*. [online]. Retrieved October 26, 2025, from https://publish.illinois.edu/infodemic/

Arar, K., & Chen, D. (2021). The future of higher education: A new paradigm shift addressing students' diversity. In H. van't Land, A. Corcoran, & D. C. Iancu (Eds.), *The promise of higher education*. Springer. https://doi.org/10.1007/978-3-030-67245-4_55

bin Mohamed, M. Z., Hidayat, R., binti Suhaizi, N. N., bin Mahmud, M. K. H., & binti Baharuddin, S. N. (2022). Artificial intelligence in mathematics education: A systematic literature review. *International Electronic Journal of Mathematics Education*, *17*(3), em0694.

Chan, C. K. Y., & Tsi, L. H. (2023). *The AI revolution in education: Will AI replace or assist teachers in higher education?* arXiv preprint arXiv:2305.01185

Chu, T. S., & Ashraf, M. (2025). Artificial intelligence in curriculum design: A data-driven approach to higher education innovation. *Knowledge*, *5*(3), 14. https://doi.org/10.3390/knowledge5030014

Crompton, H., & Burke, D. (2023). Artificial intelligence in higher education: the state of the field. *International Journal of Educational Technology in Higher Education*, *20*(1), 22.

Deepshikha, D. (2025). A comprehensive review of AI-powered grading and tailored feedback in universities. *Discover Artificial Intelligence*, *5*, 251. https://doi.org/10.1007/s44163-025-00517-0

Elstad, E. (2024). *AI in education: Rationale, principles, and instructional implications*. arXiv preprint arXiv:2412.12116

Faulconer, E., Griffith, J., & Gruss, A. (2021). The impact of positive feedback on student outcomes and perceptions. *Assessment & Evaluation in Higher Education*, *47*(2), 1–10.

Hao, K. (2019). China has started a grand experiment in AI education. It could reshape how the world learns. *MIT Technology Review*. Available at: https://www.technologyreview.com/2019/08/02/131198/china-squirrel-has-started-a-grand-experiment-in-ai-education-it-could-reshape-how-the/

Hooda, M., Rana, C., Dahiya, O., Rizwan, A., & Hossain, M. (2022). Artificial intelligence for assessment and feedback to enhance student success in higher education. *Mathematical Problems in Engineering*, *2022*, 1–19.

Jaramillo, J. J., & Chiappe, A. (2024). The AI-driven classroom: A review of 21st century curriculum trends. *Prospects*, *54*, 645–660. https://doi.org/10.1007/s11125-024-09704-w.

Lopez-Gazpio, I. (2025). Integrating large language models into accessible and inclusive education: Access democratization and individualized learning enhancement supported by generative artificial intelligence. *Information*, *16*(6), 473. https://doi.org/10.3390/info16060473.

MOOC Courses. (2022). *Search thousands of courses from top universities.* [online] Edukatico.org. Retrieved October 26, 2025, from https://www.edukatico.org/en/report/mooc-courses-search-thousands-of-courses-from-top-universities

Murniarti, E., & Siahaan, G. (2025). The synergy between artificial intelligence (AI) and experiential learning in enhancing students' creativity through motivation. In *Frontiers in education* (Vol. 10, p. 1606044). Frontiers.

Navas Bonilla, C. D. R., Viñan Carrasco, L. M., Gaibor Pupiales, J. C., & Murillo Noriega, D. E. (2025). The future of education: A systematic literature review of self-directed learning with AI. *Future Internet*, *17*(8), 366. https://doi.org/10.3390/fi17080366

Nunes, D., & Antunes, L. (2024). *Machines of meaning*. arXiv preprint arXiv:2412.07975

Peng, J., & Li, Y. (2025). Frontiers of artificial intelligence for personalized learning in higher education: A systematic review of leading articles. *Applied Sciences*, *15*(18), 10096. https://doi.org/10.3390/app151810096

Ruziev, E. (2025). AI and the future of teacher roles: Automation vs. augmentation. *Journal of Multidisciplinary Bulletin*, *8*(1), 51–54.

Salloum, S. A., Alomari, K. M., Alfaisal, A. M. et al. (2025). Emotion recognition for enhanced learning: Using AI to detect students' emotions and adjust teaching methods. *Smart Learning Environments*, *12*, 21. https://doi.org/10.1186/s40561-025-00374-5

Schiff, D. (2021). Out of the laboratory and into the classroom: The future of artificial intelligence in education. *AI & Society*, *36*, 331–348. https://doi.org/10.1007/s00146-020-01033-8

Shah, D., Pickard, L., & Ma, R. (2022). *Massive list of MOOC platforms around the world in 2022.* [online] The Report by Class Central. Retrieved October 26, 2025, from https://www.classcentral.com/report/mooc-platforms/

Shahzad, M. F., Xu, S., & Javed, I. (2024). ChatGPT awareness, acceptance, and adoption in higher education: The role of trust as a cornerstone. *International Journal of Educational Technology in Higher Education*, *21*, 46. https://doi.org/10.1186/s41239-024-00478-x

Sparrow, R., & Flenady, G. (2025). Bullshit universities: The future of automated education. *AI & Society*, *40*, 5285–5296. https://doi.org/10.1007/s00146-025-02340-8

Villegas-Ch, W., Buenano-Fernandez, D., Navarro, A. M., & Mera-Navarrete, A. (2025). Adaptive intelligent tutoring systems for STEM education: Analysis of the learning impact and effectiveness of personalized feedback. *Smart Learning Environments*, *12*, 41. https://doi.org/10.1186/s40561-025-00389-y

Made in the USA
Monee, IL
12 November 2026

8ce961c4-7c64-486c-af71-c8749ceb4d16R01